83 Changes in 17 Months

83 Changes in 17 Months

Ninan P Chandy

First Printing, 2025

CONTENTS

ACKNOWLEDGMENTS

Because no journey worth remembering is ever walked alone.

As I look back on this extraordinary journey, the challenges, the breakthroughs, the uncertainties, the moments of joy- one truth stands out above everything else:

I did not walk this path alone. Every step was guided, supported, strengthened, and blessed by the Almighty and people around me.

To God Almighty

My deepest gratitude is to God Almighty, whose divine presence lit the way even when I could not see the path clearly. Every decision, every change, every success carried a touch of grace far beyond my capability. Without His powerful hand over me, none of this would have been possible.

And to my beloved parents, who watch over me from heaven - your blessings continue to hold me upright in every storm.

To My Family My Strength Behind the Scenes

To my wife, Sherly, whose unwavering support was the anchor of my daily life. She woke up well before sunrise, preparing my breakfast and lunch by 6:30 a.m., knowing how long the day ahead would be. She bore my absence on weekends with quiet patience. She endured the strain without a word of complaint. Her sacrifices formed the invisible backbone of this journey.

To my daughter, Christina, who understood the demands on my time and never burdened me with her own. Her silent maturity and love made even the toughest days lighter.

My victories were theirs long before they were mine.

To My Mentors and Superiors - The Architects of this Opportunity

My heartfelt appreciation to the top management of Al Babtain Power and Telecom Co. Riyadh- Mr. Ibrahim Al Babtain, Chairman, Mr. Wissa Michael, CEO, Mr. Abdul Aziz Al Wuhaibi, GM, Mr. Jawad Shahedah, DGM, Mr. Tamer Kalo, Marketing & Sales Manager

Thank you for trusting me, a person from a non-factory background to lead a manufacturing organisation through its most crucial transformation.

You approved my requests without hesitation, appreciated the results openly, forgave my mistakes graciously, and stood by me during difficult moments. What you gave me was more than authority, you gave me freedom, courage, and belief.

Your leadership made this journey not just successful, but meaningful.

To My Colleagues the Heart and Hands of ALCO

To my colleagues at ALCO, who turned every idea into action: Mr. Venkatesh, Operations Manager, Mr. Unnikrishnan, Maintenance Head, Mr. Basheer, Design Head , Mr. Prabhakaran, Welder to name a few .

You were the warriors on the ground. You executed every change, every repair, every innovation with commitment and pride. ALCO's transformation was not the result of one leader — it was the result of a united team determined to rise together.

My gratitude extends to *every single employee*, from helpers to supervisors to engineers. Each of you contributed in ways big and small, and none of it went unnoticed.

To the Team That Brought This Book to Life

My sincere thanks to Mr. Hemsingh Patle and Mr. Manoj Sonawane, my publishing team, BLISS Books editorial, for shaping and refining the manuscript, Mr. Krishnamurthy P, MD of Aura, Chennai, for encouraging me to publish this experience, Mr. Sajan Geevarghese, my fellow PhD scholar, for bringing the scenario to life with his sketches

If any name has been unintentionally left out, know that your contribution is still deeply appreciated. Turning around an organisation is never the achievement of one person; it is a symphony where every player matters.

To all of you, thank you.

From the deepest corners of my heart thank you.

Without you, this story would have remained untold.

With you, it became unforgettable.

Dear Chandy,

It is wonderful to hear this from you.

Congratulations, that period at ALCO was a remarkable time of transformation, and I am pleased to see those efforts documented and shared in this book.

Thank you very much for your kind words and for acknowledging my support in the book. It was a pleasure working with you during such a pivotal time for the company.

I wish you great success with the book and all your future endeavors.

-Mr. Jawad Shehadeh, CEO, Al Babtain Power and Telecom Co., Riyadh, Kingdom of Saudi Arabia.

If you manage people or processes, this book is gold. The transformation feels human, not corporate. An outstanding real-world case study documented in this book.

-Mr.Manoj Sonawane, Author of the book Learning 2.0/Knowledgepreneur /Book Strategist /Mentor to Visionary Authors

This is not just a turnaround story—it's a leadership philosophy in action. The honesty and humility of the journey are rare. I strongly recommended this book to anyone who truly wants to create meaningful change in their work.

-Mr.Hemsingh Patle, author of the book The 5-Minute Magical Habits.

FOREWORD

Every once in a while, a story emerges from the corporate world that reminds us why leadership still matters, why people still make the difference, and why extraordinary transformations can come from the most unexpected places and people. This book — *83 Changes in 17 Months: A True Story of Transforming a Struggling Factory into a 5.7x Profit Powerhouse* is one such gem.

This book chronicles how an organisation on the brink, found its strength again — not through complex systems or expensive interventions, but through relentless observation, decisive actions, and unwavering belief in people. Opportunities and Shortcomings are identified and acted upon promptly. What transpired is nothing short of remarkable.

This book is not merely meant to be read —it is meant to be acted upon.

The pace of change, averaging 5 per month and 12 in Oct 2009 alone is mind boggling. These 83 changes contain every type of Management philosophies and practises -Lean, TOC, Six Sigma, 5S, Kaizen , TQM ,TPM, SCOR etc - put into action without prior knowledge. It was common sense of a lot of people, joining hands for a good cause – improve the company.

The Financial results were the most impressive – Revenues grew 40% YoY and Profits grew 570% YoY - achieved without Capex or Downsizing .This is only a reflection of something far deeper: The factory had rediscovered its heart. The financial results were not the objective of changes; it was a natural by-product.

Never before have I come across a book on Organisational improvement focus on Human welfare as this one. So many changes to improve the life and income of the main resource - the Human Resource . Environment ,Wastes , Sustainability were all addressed before improving the product or process .

Constraints are identified and broken over several attempts, the changes implemented in a step-by-step manner . This resulted in a growth which was organic and permanent rather than radical and transient .

But beyond all numbers and milestones, the real magic of this journey lies in the **spirit** in which it unfolded. It is a journey where:

- Human welfare weighed more than profits .
- Constraints conjured abundance
- Waste became a source of funds for employee welfare.
- Adversity was turned into improvement opportunities

This book is more than a turnaround manual. It is a handbook of actions and ideas . It is a reminder that **organisational transformation does not begin with technology, tools, or consultants — it begins with people.** With respect for them, belief in them, and empowerment of them.

For every entrepreneur who feels stuck, for every manager who feels overwhelmed, for every leader who wonders how to drive change without disrupting — this book offers hope, clarity, and a roadmap built on lived experience.

As you move from change to change - 83 in all , you will walk through the uncertainties , the struggles, the decisions, the breakthroughs, and the quiet victories that shaped ALCO's rebirth. You will see the power of small changes done consistently. You will feel the heartbeat of a factory learning to believe in itself again.

And perhaps, you will discover the spark of transformation within your own organisation.

I congratulate the author for documenting this remarkable journey with honesty, humility, and heart. May this book guide you, dear readers, inspire you, and remind you that **change — real change — is possible and begins with a single step, taken with good intention.**

Wish your Enterprise transform. rise up, adding value to the economy and all stake holders- Owners, Customers, Suppliers, Employees, Society and Environment.

— Mr. Krishnamurthy P, MD of Aura Industrial Equipment and Projects Pvt Ltd, Chennai

1

Introduction

When a Company Stands at a Crossroad...

Every business, at least once in its lifetime, finds itself standing at a crossroad, a moment where it must choose between slow decline or courageous transformation.

In mid-2009, Al-Babtain Lighting Company (ALCO) found itself exactly at that point. But it chose courageous transformation. The CEO assigned Mr. Ninan P Chandy, then Exports Sales Manager of the group to oversee ALCO's performance for a month and submit a report on how it can be improved. The report was submitted in end Aug and formed the blue print of what happened there after.

This book is the story of how a 25-year-old organisation, with 150 hardworking employees and a legacy of strength, responded when destiny knocked. It captures — month by month — the 83 actions taken that lifted ALCO from uncertainty to an extraordinary turnaround, increasing net profit by an unbelievable 570% in the very next year.

And no ,this was not a temporary miracle.

It was not luck. It was not a flash in the pan. The growth continued. The profits sustained. And the culture transformed.

The Unlikely Leader

What makes this journey even more compelling is that it was led by someone with no manufacturing background. An outsider.

A non-factory person. Someone unburdened by "how things were always done."

This is not a book of theories. No Lean. No TOC. No Six Sigma. No endless meetings, complicated analysis, simulations, or thick presentations. This is a book of pure action. Relentless, fearless, daily action. One small improvement at a time, one area or another. Revisiting the areas to unearth more One decision at a time. One belief: *"We can do better, anywhere, everywhere."*

The Power of First-Time Actions

Only first-time initiatives and meaningful changes have been chronicled here. Changes in process, system, structure, layout, planning, housekeeping, ordering, communication, and countless small but powerful shifts.

The results were staggering:

- Higher top line
- Higher bottom line
- Improved On-time delivery
- Higher STR
- Faster turnaround time
- Lower consumptions
- Higher Production
- Minimum scrap
- And above all, a united, energized workforce whose morale skyrocketed

These outcomes were never the objective. They were simply the result of doing the right things consistently and courageously.

No behavioural change program was even envisaged because forcing behaviour change breeds resistance. Instead, when systems changed, behaviour changed to suit the new set up.

Why This Book Matters to You

The ideas shared here are universal. They are applicable to any industry, any age , any size. The truth is that Longevity of any company can be improved by improving its financial performance.

Many companies are on a leash today ,struggling with rising costs, static prices, shrinking margins, frustrated employees, the fear of touching anything for fear of breaking everything.

This book is a reminder, a guide, and a reassurance that change is possible, change is practical, change is powerful. And change begins with one action not one presentation. At the end of each chapter, you will find a simple, practical page to help you:

- Implement the ideas
- Record your own changes
- Track progress
- Build momentum
- And turn your organisation into a continuous-improvement engine

This book is dedicated to every entrepreneur who wakes up each morning, to build something better, to create value, to employ people, to fight another battle and to dream of a stronger future. May this book give you the courage to challenge the status quo. May it inspire you to act boldly, consistently, relentlessly. And may it strengthen your belief that turnarounds are not miracles... they are decisions.

If at any point you wish to discuss ideas, share your journey, or seek guidance, connect me here: Email:**ninanchandy@deltaeta.in** Mobile: **+91 77360 88076** or at **www.deltaeta.in**, Thank you for ordering this book. Thank you for believing in improvement. And thank you for choosing to begin your own transformative journey.

Happy reading.
Ninan P. Chandy

2

A Brief About ALCO

To understand the magnitude of ALCO's turnaround, lets understand the company itself, its roots, its challenges, and the sheer complexity of what it was trying to build in 2009.

Al-Babtain Lighting Company (ALCO) was founded in 1984 by the visionary Al-Babtain family in Riyadh. It was born as a natural extension of their thriving High Mast and Pole Factory, a move to complete the ecosystem of outdoor lighting solutions. The company earned its ISO 9001 certification in 1996, a proud milestone in its journey toward quality excellence.

Yet, by 2009, ALCO wasn't shining as brightly as its heritage suggested.

While other group companies galloped ahead, ALCO seemed to limp behind , steady in turnover, but painfully fragile in profitability. Even after touching a new high in sales in 2008, the bottom line stubbornly hovered around 4%, and the first six months of 2009 offered no relief.

It was a company rich in potential, yet struggling to convert it into performance.

A Factory Full of Strength

Nestled in Riyadh's Second Industrial Area, ALCO's factory stood proudly on a 150m × 80m plot, with a covered structure of 120m × 70m. Within those walls lived extraordinary capabilities, the kind most companies only dream of.

ALCO wasn't just assembling products. It was creating them, end-to-end.

Its intellectual capital included the engineering expertise to design:

- Lighting system for Highways, Tunnels, and Service roads
- Lighting system for Olympic Stadiums with live TV coverage
- Lighting System for Airports, Sea ports, large areas
- Post installation lighting and performance verification (PILPV)
- Complex reflectors
- Luminaires and Floodlights ranging from 70W to a powerful 2000W
- Customised LV distribution boards
- IP protection as demanded

Its physical capabilities were even more impressive:

- Fabrication shop
- CNC machining centres
- Large presses , Spinning units
- Hi-Pressure die casting Aluminium foundry
- Electrostatic painting line on a conveyor with 120 hangers
- Anodizing unit
- Mechanical and electrical assembly lines
- A world-class IP (Ingress Protection) lab
- A fully equipped electrical testing laboratory
- Multiple warehouses
- R& D centre with model making facility

This was a factory built not on convenience, but on craftsmanship. Across the years, ALCO earned certifications from SASO and KEMA, building credibility across the Middle East, Asia , Africa, Europe and far beyond supplying quality products to over 25 countries.

A Product Universe That Could Overwhelm Even the Best

To work at ALCO was to stand inside a universe of endless combinations. With:

- 55 + luminaire models
- 5 + electrical operating conditions (220/230/240/380/415 V, 50/60Hz)
- 3 lamp types (HPMV, HPSV, MH) + Halogen
- Lamp wattages – 70w,125w,150w,250w,400w,600w,1000wand 2000w+500w Halogen.

...the permutations and combinations were not just many, they were mind-boggling. And unlike mass manufacturers, ALCO built every single product to order. No stock. No shortcuts. Every fitting was a custom response to a customer's unique requirement. In short, ALCO had immense capability, enormous complexity, and incredible potential. What it lacked was alignment, flow, coordination, and a system that allowed all these strengths to work together rather than pull apart. This was the stage. This was the canvas. This was the company waiting for transformation. And this is where the story began.

3

The Storm That Cleared the Path

Month 1 – August 2009

Paulo Coelho wrote in The Alchemist, *"When you want something, all the universe conspires in helping you to achieve it."* That line came true at ALCO as everyone wanted it to do well .

Change #1: A Strategic Leap of Faith

The very first change at ALCO wasn't operational. It wasn't technical. It was strategic. Top management took a bold step, they appointed a non-factory person to head ALCO. For decades, ALCO had been managed by Factory managers, highly qualified engineers who had spent their lives in manufacturing functions. They had worked tirelessly to develop the product line, improve infrastructure, secure certifications, and bring ALCO to its current level. Their contribution was foundational.

Yet, despite increasing turnover until 2008, profitability remained stubbornly low. That's when management decided to take a risk. They chose someone who came without the baggage of factory norms, someone unbound by habit, history, or limiting beliefs. It was like the bumble bee, which flies not knowing that technically it cannot, due to its weight and short wings. I walked in unaware of perceived limitations, free from the prison of "this is how we've always done it". Top management supported me fully, never questioning a decision, never denying a request, never withholding funds. Sometimes, the greatest breakthroughs happen when a leader enters with the freedom to dream differently.

Change #2: When You Decide to Change, Embrace It Fully

Once recommendations from the initial study were approved, they were implemented completely. Organizational structure was changed , The Chief's title changed from "Factory Manager" to Business Unit Head (BUH), reflecting broader responsibility and true P&L ownership.

ISO 9001 procedures were revised immediately to align with the new structure. The new BUH was relieved from previous responsibilities, so full focus could be directed toward ALCO. Interestingly, "BUH" already existed in the company at a section head level , but only as a *responsibility without authority*.

Change #3: Some Storms Come to Clear the Path

29th August 2009

Reached ALCO in the Second Industrial Area on the outskirts of Riyadh city by 7.30am It was the holy month of Ramadan . At 10:00 a.m., called a meeting of all the staff and supervisors- around 25 . A few of them were familiar faces, though I had not worked with any of them before .Many knew me due to my long tenure in the company and as past Chairman of the Al Babtain Sports Committee . By 11:30 a.m., took a round of the shop floor and premises with the Operations Manager (OM).

Material... Material Everywhere

The inside and outside (all four sides) of the factory were filled with material, making it difficult to navigate our way through. Inside, the space was packed with raw materials, work-in-progress items, and finished goods. Outside the building, the area was cluttered with discarded racks, scrap, debris, pipes, rejected items, broken pallets, old machines, and some freshly arrived materials . A container load had arrived the previous week, but there was no place to store it inside , so was stored outside.

The Arabian summer was at its peak ,scorching hot, dry, and intensely bright . Yet the shop floor was surprisingly dark. Dust covered most of the items, and even the entire array of illuminated high-bay luminaires, each fitted with 400-watt High-pressure Metal halide lamps, was not enough to brighten the floor. A luminaire factory in darkness .What an irony!

Accustomed to the neat, clean, and well-lit ambience of the head office, this sight was far from pleasing. I resolved to do something about it in due course, although at that moment, I had no idea how to begin or where to start. By late afternoon, the universe sent its first sign and it came in the form of a storm on paper. An Arabic letter arrived from the Industrial Estate Authorities. Attached to it was a handwritten note in English from my boss. It was a penalty letter. The offense? Not maintaining the 5-meter clear passage around the factory, as required by law.

The letter also served a warning that if the same offense was repeated, more stringent action could be expected. It advised us to clear all materials and maintain the 5-meter passage around the factory at all times. Although no specific deadline was mentioned, it was clear that an inspection could happen at any time, as officers in uniform were specifically assigned to monitor the Industrial Estate. They regularly patrolled the area in jeeps, taking photographs of violations and they performed their duties with sincerity. Offenses such as loading or unloading materials outside the premises, littering, or allowing waste water to overflow beyond the boundary were closely monitored and penalized.

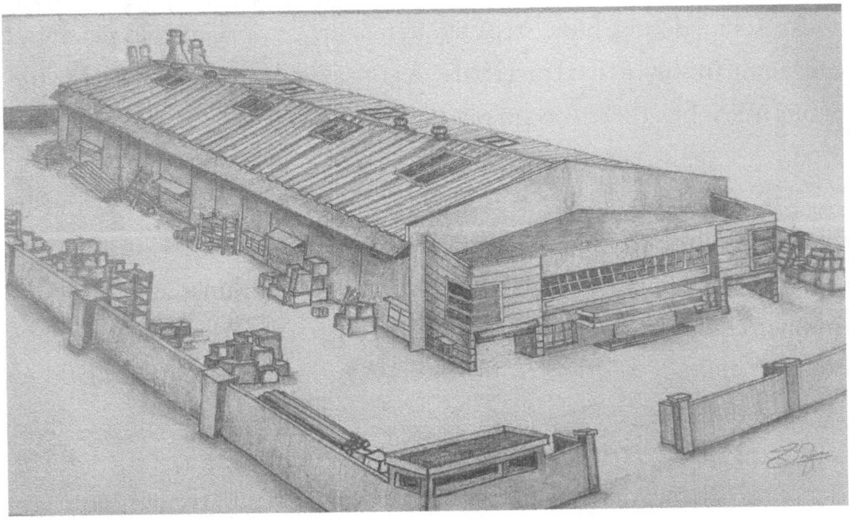

Figure 1: An artist's view of factory on 29th Aug 2009

Discussed the matter with the Operations Manager, who explained that space has been a major constraint for years. Even a separate warehouse, located 50 kilometres away , hired lately to ease this problem, was already overflowing. Many attempts had been made in the past to manage the situation, but nothing worked because of the large variety and volume of materials. As per the Industrial Estate Authority's regulations, a 5-meter open space had to be maintained on all sides of the building to allow the free movement of fire engines. Unfortunately ,it was not maintained free and the authorities were prompt to point out .

The two of us went around the factory once again to assess the type and quantity of material lying around. After that, called the Stores Head (SH) and Maintenance Head (MH) to the meeting room for an emergency discussion. I shared the letter with them and sought their suggestions on how to prevent such an incident from recurring. The group collectively agreed on a two-day timeframe to set things right, as the Saudi authorities could revisit the premises anytime in early September.

August 29 was a Saturday, and we agreed to go at full throttle. Stores Head was assigned the responsibility of moving all raw materials from outside to inside the factory, while Maintenance Head was tasked with shifting all other items to the distant warehouse or discarding whatever was no longer needed. We all agreed to stay late if required to complete the task.

The Operations Manager was assigned the responsibility of providing all the necessary resources available within the factory, while I took charge of arranging any additional support required from outside. Other group companies had trailers, cranes, and similar equipment at their disposal, which we could access at arm's length but the real challenge was ensuring prompt availability. Work began immediately, on a war footing, and the sheer scale of the task turned out to be far greater than what we had anticipated.

The clearance job was like vacating a house; as we kept clearing things out, more materials kept appearing. To keep the workers comfortable, soft drinks, water, and snacks were provided regularly in a separate area (since eating in public is not permitted during the fasting hours of Ramadan). The temperature was around 50°C, yet the team worked tirelessly.

By the evening of the 31st, the passage around the entire factory was completely cleared, marking the beginning of a transformative journey. More than the satisfaction of the cleanup itself, the greatest reward was that we completed the task within the estimated time and the team's estimate had proven to be remarkably accurate.

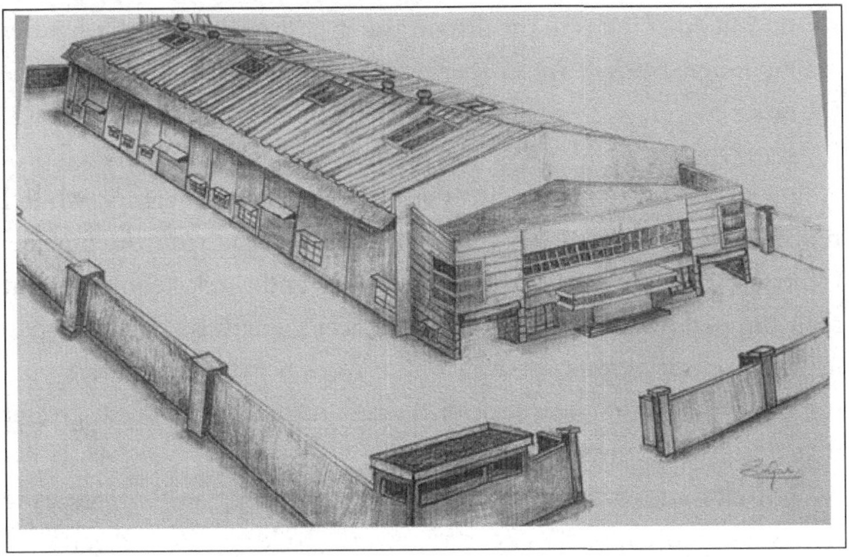

Figure 2: Artist's View of the factory on 31 Aug 2009

Key learnings:

1. To achieve a new result, a new way must be tried
2. An external threat can also be an opportunity
3. A problem shared leads to faster problem-solving
4. Assign tasks in areas under their jurisdiction.

Reflection:

It was a good start, better than I had ever imagined. Never did I expect the entire premises to be cleared in just two days.

In hindsight, that penalty letter was perhaps the best thing that could have happened. It was not punishment; it was a push from the universe.

If the warning hadn't come, we might still be waiting for the "right time" to begin. But that urgency, that fear, united us. It triggered something primal, the fight or flight response and we chose to fight together.

As I stood in the quiet factory yard that night, I looked around at the cleared space and smiled. Maybe Coelho was right... And this was just the beginning.

4

The Month of Awakening

Month 2 – September 2009
Increasing Capacity by 10% Without Capex

The transformation had begun. The miraculous cleanup in the last two days of August had brought not just order to the premises, it had also brought hope. What was thought impossible had been achieved in just two days. The factory that once looked like a scrapyard now had breathing space.

Will it last was the silent question in everybody's mind .Or, is it the case of a new broom ...

Yes, deep down, I knew this victory could easily fade. This time, it had to be different. The real change needed to go deeper into the mindset, the systems, and the culture. With that resolve ,started the month ,still unsure of what next !

Understanding the Numbers

Al-Babtain Power & Telecom had a system of every factory submitting its monthly performance based on stock movement, deliveries, and expenses. A standard format existed, supported by ERP data. The Operations Manager prepared ALCO's report for August, and there was little to celebrate, but plenty to learn.

Spent my days going through records, order books, customer complaints, delivery histories, employee details, and ordering patterns. Being an ISO 9001 certified company ,it had its perks, everything was documented and records were available .

With each file reviewed and each factory walk I took, one truth became clearer: ALCO was not failing because of people or process , it was failing because of unsynchronised effort.

So, started making a list of all activities that needed change to sync .

Change #4: A Seat That Changed Perspective - Pragmatism, Not Feng Shui or Vaastu

My office was on the first floor, facing the door. The factory lay behind me, hidden from sight, separated by a window covered in dust and cobwebs. Every few minutes, I found myself standing up, turning around, trying to see where a noise came from or what activity was happening.

After a few sit ups, decided to turn my desk 90 degrees to face the factory directly from the seat . The windows were cleaned, and clear view replaced the gloom. From my new seat, I could see the entire shop floor. Visitors, too, could witness operations in action as their seat positions was also changed . The change improved observation, and brought a sense of openness and connection. I didn't have to rely on third party for information: I was a witness to most happenings.

It wasn't Feng Shui or Vaastu , it was practical.

Change #5: The Paradigm Shift - From Production to Delivery

When the official P&L arrived, calculated the factory's breakeven point (BEP) , roughly SR 3 million in monthly deliveries. For the first time, realized that profitability depended solely on dispatched goods, not production.

Production without delivery was merely inventory, not revenue.

After reviewing the numbers with the Operations Manager, we identified three levers to improve profits: Price, Quantity dispatched and

Cost. Price hikes were unrealistic, and cost reduction would take time. That left only one lever -increasing the quantity dispatched .

With about SR 10 million in backlogged orders and finished goods piling up, I instructed the team to target SR 5 million or more in deliveries from stock and fresh production .

From that day, the objective of the factory shifted from production to dispatch.

Production was no longer about what could be made; it was about what could be delivered.

The change in focus was simple yet revolutionary. We revised daily reports to highlight "Ready Orders Awaiting Release." Sales and factory teams began working in sync. Finished goods started moving. For the first time in months, the Finished Goods warehouse was breathing again.

Change #6: Fostering Relationships - Iftar at ALCO

Around the second week of September, with the holy month of Ramadan in its second phase, asked the Operations Manager whether ALCO had ever hosted an Iftar for its employees. He smiled politely and said "No". Only the Chairman of the group hosts for senior executives."

We planned an Iftar for **09-09-2009**, coincidentally the same day the Dubai Metro was inaugurated, a day symbolic of progress. The budget was approved instantly. Our IT Head took charge of coordination and, he executed it beautifully.

No one knew what to expect. It was the first time such an event had been held at ALCO. We invited managers from sister companies, engineers from Sales and Purchase, suppliers, and service providers. Food was ordered from a well-known restaurant. Seating was arranged in groups of eight along the T-shaped passage of the shop floor.

Everyone contributed to cleaning and decorating the factory. Passages were vacuumed, desert coolers and fans were hired, and tables and chairs were arranged. Some employees made a handmade "Welcome" sign using thermocol sheets. Shifts were adjusted so all employees and contract staff could attend.

The break of fast was signalled around 5.40pm .The aroma of food mixed with gratitude. Cameras clicked, smiles spread, and laughter echoed through the factory. There was no separate area for managers or guests. Everyone shared the same food; seats were not reserved and the guests mingled with all. Non-Muslims gave preference to their Muslim brothers as they were fasting since day break .

Three former ALCO Factory Managers attended as guests. Someone joked, "It's like M. S. Dhoni (Former Captain of the Indian Cricket Team) leading the Indian team with three ex-captains beside him."

That evening, ALCO didn't feel like a factory. It felt like a family.

After prayers, guests toured the premises and were astonished to see the clean surroundings, the organized floor, the fresh energy. The evening left an impression on everyone. Soon after, our sister companies began hosting their own Iftars.

It was not just a celebration; it felt like a family coming together.

Change #7: Closer Surveillance Through CCTV

My predecessor had ordered a CCTV system, and it was installed during Ramadan days . Eight cameras ,some with zooming facility ,now covered all key areas: The Operations Manager, security cabin , and I had the monitors.

For the first time, every movement inside and outside the factory could be observed transparently. Employees, too, became aware that the cameras were recording. Dumping of material outside stopped completely. Discipline improved .

With this and my new desk position, the entire factory was under clear view not for policing, but for accountability.

Change #8: Moving Setup Time Outside the Shift

One morning, while checking the CCTV feed, noticed no activity in the painting shop . The crew was present, yet there was no object loading . I went down immediately, fearing a breakdown , for which the painting line was notoriously famous

It wasn't a breakdown; it was standard practise . The team was waiting for the curing oven to heat up, a process that took 30 minutes. The same delay occurred at the end of every shift for cooling. In effect, an hour of production time was lost every day.

Later , after long discussions with the Operation Manager , production engineer, supervisor, and painters, facing their fair share of resistance, we decided to try a new system. The supervisor would arrive 30 minutes early and leave 30 minutes late, in a dedicated vehicle.

That simple change moved the setup time outside the production shift.

The results were stunning:

Shift Duration	Setup Time	Rounds/ Shift	Output/ Day
11 hours	1 hour	5.0	600 pieces
11 hours	0 hour	5.5	660 pieces

A 10% increase in output without a single rupee of capital expenditure. It was our first real productivity gain, a small step that boosted confidence across the floor.

Change #9: Establishing a Disagreement Mechanism

During that same discussion, I noticed something deeper. Whenever a new idea was proposed, the standard reply was:
"It hasn't been done before," or "It can't be done."

This mindset was the biggest bottleneck.

Once the painting line results spoke for themselves, used that success as proof. Issued a simple but powerful circular:

"Any disagreement with a proposed change must be submitted in writing, with a valid reason and an alternative proposal ."

This simple rule ended arguments on the shop floor. Frivolous objections ended . Well intended written objections received were reviewed , discussed with the originator and many a times better alternatives than original suggestion emerged. This mechanism became a template for all future changes.

Change #10: Cobweb-Free Factory

The CCTV revealed something we'd never noticed: cobwebs hanging from the ceiling beams, and trusses. They looked terrible on the monitor, a symbolic layer of neglect.

We decided to act. With Ramadan's reduced working hours, we used the extra time of the contract staff to clean every inch above eye level.A tall maintenance ladder was repaired, reinforced, and fitted with safety brakes and stays. A custodian was assigned for safe supervision, and the ladder got its designated place.

When the ceilings shone clean and walls gleamed, the transformation was more than physical, it was psychological. With improved housekeeping, employees started maintaining their areas pro-actively.

Continuation of Change #5: The Delivery-First Mindset

After Ramadan holidays, the factory reopened in the last week of September. The production plan for October targeting SR 3.0 million was prepared and sent to me for approval.

I returned it with a note: *"Revise target to meet SR 5 million in delivery . Let's break the ceiling."*

The team was shocked that this figure had been reached only two or three times in ALCO's 25-year history.

I shared the breakeven analysis again. Everyone understood why profits were poor; most months had deliveries below SR 3 million. The focus shifted entirely to delivery.

We identified "Ready Orders Awaiting Release", and the planner began filtering deliverable ones. Sales was asked to pressurise customers and send release orders more efficiently. Material from the factory were dispatched only on receipt of Release order from Sales , another good practise at Babtain.

For the first time, Sales and Factory stopped blaming each other and started collaborating. The old *silo mentality* broke down. The factory's new purpose became clear: Deliver, not just produce.

Key Learnings:

1. A monthly P&L is like a milestone marker — it tells you how far you've really gone.
2. A celebration brings people together; joy is infectious.
3. Aim high, even if it's never been achieved before — there's always a first time.
4. Setup time eats production time — move it outside the shift.

Reflection:

September was short with fewer working days, shorter hours yet seven meaningful changes took place.

The Iftar created unity and pride. The CCTV system paid for itself within a month through higher output and improved cleanliness. The mindset began to shift from *excuses* to *execution*.

The team was learning, adapting, believing. ALCO was finally waking up.

By the end of September, something remarkable had happened. For the first time, people at ALCO started saying "Let's try it" instead of "It can't be done." That single change from doubt to determination was the spark that would light up the months ahead.

5

Building a Workplace That Cares

Month 3 – October 2009

One full month since taking charge, and I was still unsure of what to do. October was the first month with full working days—an opportunity to truly test the pulse of ALCO. It had to perform, both operationally and financially.

But as I walked through the shop floor, three things demanded immediate attention:

1. Material scattered everywhere
2. Waste disposal and scrap management
3. The dark, gloomy shop floor

I made a mental note; these would be my priorities. I didn't yet know it, but October would become the month of transformation.

Change #11: Arrive Early, Leave Early

The industrial area started at 7:30 am with most companies following 7.30 to 4.30 timings.

Traffic after 7.15 was unbearable as everyone tried to reach ON TIME . Noticed something: If I left home just 30 minutes earlier, the roads were empty, smooth, and peaceful. So got permission from DGM to start early and leave early .

Reaching ALCO by 7:00 am was a joy. A 30 km drive took 20-25 minutes instead of a stressful one-hour ordeal.

Within a week, something surprising happened: Most of the staff began arriving on time too.

We introduced flexible timing:

- Come early → leave early
- But staying late → *no* excuse for arriving late

It set a quiet discipline across the organisation. Punctuality became effortless not enforced.

Change #12: Sharing Performance with Shop Floor Employees

September's delivery was below breakeven. Whatever small profit existed at the beginning of the month, just evaporated. When the accounts report arrived, I called all supervisors and above for a meeting. It was just the second general meeting since I arrived. The reaction was immediate and painful. Employees who believed they were giving their best suddenly saw the numbers. Nine months of effort. Zero profit. Just three months left. Increments at risk. Jobs possibly at risk. I told them plainly: *"If this continues, ALCO will soon be history. We may all need to look for new jobs."* Silence filled the room. A heavy, honest silence. Then I opened the floor with a question *"What do you think we should do?"*

The answers came tumbling out:

- Production: *"We can produce ... if material comes on time."*
- PPC: *"We can plan . if purchase follows."*
- All: *"Interruptions kill us."*
- Others: *"Finished goods are blocking space ."*

Everyone was right in their own way. I assured them: *"My door is open. We will solve these issues together."* Then I shared a basic truth: *"Profit is not made when we produce. Profit is realised only when the material leaves the gate and an invoice is raised".* With three months left for the year to close , asked them to chase something ALCO had never done consistently: **5 million riyals delivery every month.** A new benchmark. A new ambition. A new collective dream.

Change #13: Aging Bucket for Stock

In finance, an aging bucket helps track overdue receivables and we at sales were familiar with it. I needed the same but for Stock.

ALCO's IT department prepared the Aging Bucket for Finished Goods. Some orders were lying for over a year.

Took appointment to meet my previous boss, the Sales & Marketing Manager over coffee at the Head Office the next day. As H.O was between my home and the factory , visited only while going or coming back and seldom was asked to come in between.

Sales managers and Sales coordinators were invited by Sales and Marketing Manager after knowing the agenda . After pleasantries and coffee, I laid out the truth: 1) Stores overflowing, 2) Invoicing blocked, 3) Profits until Sept 30, brutally low and 4) Many old orders untouched.

We didn't waste time blaming each other. Instead, we acted. Duplicate orders were cancelled. Some orders were short-closed (even my orders were there). Customers were asked to lift material or take revise delivery dates

Sales agreed to give quick release orders for items ready and due . In one month, the aging of stock dropped dramatically. A single visit accomplished more than a dozen emails ever could.

The expired price list needed updating and Sales requested discount to compete in the market and get more orders, as a return favour. I promised to do my best .

Change #14: Objective-Based Inventory Management (STR & DSI) - A personal compass

Turning an MBA Lesson Into a Practical Lifesaver. Inventory must balance two things:

- Avoiding shortage
- Avoiding excess

But ALCO had too many SKU's and too much stock. I revisited concepts from my MBA:

- STR – Stock Turnover Ratio
- DSI- Days Sales of Inventory

The existing monthly report didn't show STR. So I calculated it myself. The number was shocking—and dangerous. I devised a modified STR to reflect real-time performance:

Modified STR = Last Month's COGS / Last month's Closing stock of raw material

And

DSI = 360 / STR

These simple formulas became powerful:

- They revealed updated inefficiencies
- They exposed excess stock
- They showed daily progress
- They became my personal whistle-blower system

A small Excel sheet became my compass. Targeted to halve it in a year from the present .

Change #15: A discounted New Price List

ALCO's price list was complicated due to:

- Many variants
- Frequent component price changes
- Currency fluctuation

Reworking it was a time-consuming nightmare. So, made a bold decision: *"Issued a revised price list with a 3% discount".* And my boss trusted me completely. Never questioned it once. Sales was happy. As they knew ALCO's situation ,appreciated the discount and pledged to do their best. For large and big tenders or projects, we always accommodated discounts. Flexibility with structure, that was our mantra.

Change #16: Sustainability Practices

Every morning, I would take a round around the factory premises to ensure that premises was clear of material and see things as they were, not how they were shown. My eyes often stopped at one spot, the large SKIP (the waste bin) parked near the dispatch gate.

It overflowed with cartons, plastics, food waste, and broken pallets. Every day, a truck came to replace it. Every day, we were paying for it, 10,000 SR per month, to be exact.

One morning, while standing there, I wondered, "Where does all this go?" The Operations Manager told me that except for steel and aluminium scrap, everything else from the factory was just thrown away.

Being a luminaire manufacturer, we received tons of packaging material -cartons, plastics, rubber , foam , crates etc Once opened, they all went straight into the SKIP along with food waste . Everything reusable or not ended up as waste.

It didn't make sense. Waste was not just waste; it was value misplaced.

Called the Operations Manager again and discussed how we could salvage. Spoke to a scrap dealer and learned something shocking: a ton of paper waste could fetch 350–400 SR, and we were generating at least that much every week! Plastics, PVC, and broken pallets all could be sold too.

Of course, there was resistance. "Production will drop," some supervisors warned, "if we start flattening every carton before disposal." But this was not about cartons ,it was about creating a culture of responsibility. So ,we acted. The new system was simple:

1. Only food waste was allowed in the general waste bin.
2. Paper, plastic, PVC, and pouches were segregated into separate bins.
3. One person was assigned to remove scrap every two hours to maintain shop floor
4. Dispatch in charge was responsible for organising the scrap sale as well as safe keeping and accounting of the funds. He did a wonderful job .

Within days, the result was visible: the SKIP that used to leave daily now left just once a week. The numbers spoke louder than words:

- Expense reduced: 7,500 SR per month
- Income from scrap sale**s:** 2,500 SR per month
- Net gain**:** 10,000 SR monthly (120,000 SR annually)

But the real gain? Cleaner floors, less clutter. A sense of pride in the workplace. And an unspoken shift in the collective mindset. We had taken our first step toward sustainability.

Benefits of this action:

- Created an income stream and reduced monthly expense.

- Encouraged recycling and responsibility
- Improved housekeeping and morale
- Minimized environmental impact

Change #17: Removing Items Not in Inventory

One afternoon, during a routine visit to the Stores, something caught my eye- an old exhibition display stand. Recognized it instantly as I had assembled and energised it at many international exhibitions all over the globe to proudly showcase our luminaires and floodlights. But now it stood there, abandoned, dusty, and forgotten.

Beside the stand, there were luminaires from foreign companies, collected as samples long ago, now serving no purpose. *"What are these doing here?"* I asked. The Stores team replied gently, *"Sir, these are not on record... all off-inventory items."* Those words opened my eyes to a silent problem- hidden clutter eating up our space, efficiency, and even morale. As we looked deeper, we found more such items scattered across the factory:

1. Fully depreciated machines
2. Old prototypes
3. Discarded tools
4. Obsolete samples
5. Forgotten fixtures

All gathering dust. We earmarked a 1-metre-wide area behind the factory and collected all such items there . It stretched to 50 metres soon. Two trailer loads were sold as scrap. Space savings: 96 +cubic metres. We regained our breathing space, both physically and operationally.

Change #18: Reduce Work in Process

With the Raw Material and Finished Goods stores becoming clutter-free, I turned my attention to the shop floor, which was crowded with Work-in-Process (WIP) materials. ALCO's products were tailor-made, built to order rather than for stock. Many work orders had been opened but were left unfinished for various reasons, creating a large number of incomplete orders that cluttered the entire shop floor.

I discussed the situation with the Operations Manager and PPC engineer to understand the root causes. We identified three main reasons:

1. Frequent changes in priority.
2. Shortage of materials.
3. Orders being put on hold indefinitely.

I suggested a strict new policy: adhere to the monthly production plan as defined in the ISO procedures, start production only when all materials are available, and review any "On Hold" orders after two weeks. After this period, a new delivery date would be set or the material would be diverted to other orders. This was communicated to all concerned departments.

Furthermore, I instructed that a maximum of only 10 work orders could be open at any given time, with no exceptions permitted. Gradually, we began to reduce the WIP, making the shop floor less cluttered. Within a month, the passages and aisles were clear of materials.

Change #19: The Employee Dining Hall

Every day during lunch, employees were seen sitting scattered in corners ,under shade, near machines, sometimes even at their workstations. It bothered me. How could we expect dignity and discipline from people if we didn't offer them a decent place to eat?

Besides, it wasn't hygienic also. Stray cats would roam around during lunchtime, and even the company dogs would show up for their right. So, decided that ALCO should have a proper dining hall.

The maintenance team was tasked with finding a space that could seat 50 people. Within ten days, a space on the first floor was cleared and transformed into a dining hall. Tables, chairs, a microwave oven , a fridge, and a water dispenser put together , they created something meaningful. The air conditioners were repaired, and the room was inaugurated with fanfare.

Lunch breaks were staggered ,so departments like Painting and Anodising didn't stop operations. For the first time, ALCO's production did not halt during lunch hours. It wasn't just about dignified eating; it was about belonging.

When employees sat together from different departments like painting, testing, assembly, they began to talk, laugh, and share stories. The "silo" mindset started breaking. Relationships formed. Energy flowed. They returned after lunch not just fed but refreshed.

Tangible benefits – Factory production time increased by 1 hour every day as there was no shutdown during lunch hours . Like shifting the set -up time in painting outside the shift ,this staggered lunch time gave another one hour every day

With an investment of SR. 10,000/ for the table and chairs and other accessories, the production time improved by a whopping 9%!

Benefits of this action:

1. Continuous operation of all departments
2. Improved inter-departmental bonding
3. Better health and relaxation during breaks

Change #20: Clean Drinking Water

Kidney stone is a common health issue in Saudi Arabia, and unfortunately, many of our employees also fall victim to it. Almost every fortnight , someone would get sick. The pain usually flared up at night, and the patient would be rushed to the nearby hospital for admission. The next morning, as we entered the factory, we were often greeted by worried faces and the same bad news. Made it a practice to visit the patients along with the Operations Manager. During one such visit, we met the duty doctor , an Egyptian who explained that the condition was primarily caused by not drinking enough water — and the only real remedy was to drink more.

It was later observed that although the company provided one potable water outlet from a tank, most employees preferred to drink water from 20-litre cans. Groups of three or four employees would purchase a can together, take a litre each for drinking, use some for making tea, and keep the remaining water locked inside their work tables. Because of the cost involved, many employees ended up restricting their water intake.

That realization hit me hard. Here we were trying to improve production and efficiency while our people were silently suffering because they couldn't afford enough drinking water.

We decided to fix it permanently.

Five hot-and-cold water dispensers were arranged by the Production Engineer , free of cost ,from the water bottle supplier, as a promotional tool . We placed them across the factory. Water cans were purchased in bulk and stored neatly. Anyone could take one.

The best part? The expense was covered from scrap sales. The waste we once paid to remove was now funding the water we gave our people. Health improved. Hospital visits dropped. Apart from improved health, the production hours also increased due to non-stoppage of work to buy the water bottles every Thursday.

Time lost = 20 minutes per group ×50 groups=1000 minutes

Frequency = Weekly once

Manhours lost/month = 1000 minutes ×4= 4000 minutes or approximately 70 man hours

Expense = 15 cans per day @2 litres per person × SR 4/can ×26= SR 1560/month

Additional Benefit of Providing Drinking Water

The washroom area in the factory used to be identifiable even from 50 meters away. Before any guests arrived to visit the shop floor, the cleaning boy would be signalled to apply lotion and fresheners to mask the odour so that it wouldn't be embarrassing. However ,The bad smell returned soon after.

After drinking water was made freely available, we noticed an unexpected benefit: the unpleasant odour gradually reduced and eventually disappeared completely.(Anyone who refrains from drinking water for 8- 12 hours can understand this phenomenon first-hand.)

To make water even more accessible, five additional water dispensers were purchased and installed across the factory so that employees didn't have to walk long distances to drink water, another small ,yet effective time-saving improvement.

And when employees saw that the water came from the money they helped earn through recycling, ownership grew, and became protectors of the system — not just participants.

Benefits of this action:

- Improved employee health
- Reduced absenteeism and hospitalisation
- Time saved and productivity gained
- Boosted satisfaction and morale

Change #21: A Kennel for the Dogs

A few years earlier, two stray puppies were adopted by the security team after an attempted break-in. The dogs became part of ALCO's family, faithful, protective, and loved by many. But as the factory grew busier and more vehicles flowed through the gate, those once-charming companions became a safety risk for visitors and a housekeeping headache.

The maintenance team was entrusted with the task of finding a place and they found a spot near the OUT gate and built a proper kennel. A desert cooler was installed so the dogs would be comfortable in the desert heat. Security was given a modest allowance to feed and care for them. Employees were asked kindly but firmly not to feed the dogs and cats inside the production area any longer, for hygiene and safety.

At first the dogs resisted the change. Who wouldn't when routines were altered. But over time they adapted, settled into their new home, and remained ALCO's guardians ,now safer, healthier, and managed with respect. This small change said something important to every employee: we care for all lives that's part of our workplace.

Change #22: Tea for All

Even after free drinking water was introduced, a chaotic tea culture persisted. Workers brewed tea in dozens of improvised spots across the shop floor. Production stopped twice per shift while groups went about their rituals of making tea. Unauthorized electrical connections created hazards; and cluttered tubs and stoves consumed space and attention. The solution was not a decree but an act of inclusion.

We centralized tea-making. After a few false starts to find a robust stove, an old German-made 2000W hot plate (two burners) from home did the trick. The "tea boy" prepared morning tea by 7:00 am and afternoon tea by 3:00 pm; night-shift arrangements were also put in place. Unauthorized kettles and cans were removed; the floor became safer and cleaner.

The results were immediate and meaningful:

- Roughly 50 tea-making groups no longer stopped work twice per shift.
- Time saved: ~500minutes/day @10 minutes per group → 216 hours/month of production time reclaimed (almost one man month)
- Cost to serve tea (estimated): ~SR 3,900/month for 150 people @0.5 SR /tea , a tiny price for enormous morale and productivity gain.

Beyond numbers, something subtler happened. Tea time moved from a secret task to a shared ritual. People met, chatted, exchanged ideas, and felt part of something kinder. The dining hall, the free water, the tea all combined into a powerful message: you matter here.

Other factories' staff, who shared accommodation with ours, noticed the difference. For the first time, they envied ALCO staff. Earlier they were treated as poor cousins!

Key Learnings:

1. Employee welfare should be a Top priority for management .
2. A strong relationship with Sales is the backbone of good factory performance.
3. Waste management is as important as production management.
4. Unaccounted material consumes space like accounted material—clean it.
5. Dining place, Tea , drinking water are not luxuries, they are basic human necessities.

Reflection

October 2009 taught me something profound: real change doesn't always need money; it needs intent. From reducing waste to creating a dining hall, from saving on expenses to improving health, each initiative stemmed from one belief: If we take care of people, factory performance will improve .

And they did. ALCO was slowly transformed from a factory into a family, from operations into a movement of purpose.

Implementation Record:

Sr. No.	Date	Reference change #	Reduce consumption of	Improve Output of	Value

6

The Month of Momentum

Month 4 – November 2009

October had closed with deliveries crossing the 5 million SR mark, a milestone that felt almost impossible just a month earlier. The internal projection estimated profits of over half a million Saudi Riyals. For a factory that was once drowning in clutter, delays, and darkness, this achievement felt nothing short of a miracle.

The next day, we celebrated with a free lunch for all employees, the first lunch party in the new dining hall, paid entirely from scrap sales. It was well deserved, as October had been a tough month with twelve changes, all closed .

Change #23: Production Bonus

Two days after the celebration, I went to the Head Office with a bold request for a special production bonus for ALCO's exceptional October performance. Bonuses of this nature were not customary in the group, and naturally, I was taken to the General Manager since it was a policy matter and my Boss supported my request.

Once the Accounts department confirmed the profit figures, my boss asked me to submit a proposal with a method of distribution. We kept it simple: the amount was based on the despatch quantity and the wattage of the fittings, while the distribution was aligned with the salary structure to avoid any ambiguity. Simple maths and it was approved without much discussion.

Everyone was to receive a share of this bonus, based on the number of days they had worked in October. I excluded myself from the recipients list . Overnight, ALCO became a sensation within the group, as no other company in the group had ever given such a bonus to shop-floor employees. Motivated by this, employees said openly, "We will beat October. We'll exceed the previous year's revenue."

And I believed them.

Change #24: Skylights: Letting the Sun Back In

Inside the factory, lighting had always felt dull, almost depressing. But there were skylights, long-forgotten, buried under thick layers of dust. No one had paid attention to them for years.

We explored ways to clean them. The Maintenance Head suggested a water-spraying company or specialized cleaners. The high roof and scorching 45°C temperature made the task risky and expensive .

Eventually, we found a group of Pakistani workers skilled in high-altitude work . Their quote was high, but we had no choice. We set this strict guideline: *No workers on the roof between 11:00 a.m. and 3:30 p.m.*

At 6 a.m. the next morning, ten men climbed up and began scraping away years of dust. By evening, the factory was bathed in natural sunlight.

For the first time, we saw ALCO as it was meant to be, bright, visible, alive. Nothing beats the sun.

Power Saved:

84 luminaires × 400W x 12 daylight hours

403 units saved per day x 360 days /year

145,080 units saved annually!!!!

Plus, longer life of lamp and control gear components reduced the replacement costs by 50%. A bright factory, lower energy bills, and a happier workforce all from one forgotten skylight.

Change #25: Introducing Job Rotation for Supervisors

Many supervisors had been in the same role for years. It breeds complacency and stagnation. I had experienced the benefits of movement myself, having worked across three product lines in my career with the group.

A circular was issued explaining the new job rotation policy and its importance for both the company and the individual. After discussing with the Operations Manager, we moved three supervisors on the shop floor and also transferred a young engineer from Maintenance to Design.

Although few raised objections and some feared that work might be affected, I reassured them that their support would be sought whenever required, and that everyone would undergo a rotation within the next six months. My case was cited as the example as everybody knew my years in sales . This assurance put all concerns to rest. Employees are happy when everybody is treated equal.

The message was clear- at ALCO, no one would remain stagnant again.

Change #26: Retiring Models That No Longer Served the Business

A deep dive into the yearly order data revealed a pattern, several models had zero orders for over a year. Market preferences had shifted to sturdier models - spun, extruded, and cast aluminium bodies.

Yet Sales insisted on retaining all the models "in case municipalities needed spares."

Instead of debating endlessly, we acted subtly. We quietly moved all dies and tools for low-performing models to the faraway warehouse, freeing up precious space .

Fortunately, not a single order for those models came until the day I left the company. The world had moved to new models..

The space gained was worth far more than the sentimental attachment to outdated products.

Change #27: Removing Siesta Joints- Reclaiming Discipline

Sunlight brought visibility not just to materials but to habits as well.

Between racks, behind shelves, under tables, we found several make shift "siesta corners," complete with cardboard beds, pillows, kettles, and even dumbbells and springs for exercise.

The next morning, a circular was issued: *No secluded resting areas allowed. Remove them voluntarily by the weekend.* Everyone complied. Discipline improved. Safety improved. An anonymous complaint came: "Why remove only from the factory? What about offices?" Fair point, we corrected that too. Leadership must begin with fairness.

Change #28: Petty Cash Purchases: The Hidden Drain on Profit

With rising production, petty cash purchases increased ,mostly small items like screws, tags, labels, ferrules, and wire end sleeves. Petty cash purchases were always practised but of late the scale had increased .

A comparison of prices shocked me with this insight: *Petty cash purchase prices were 300% to 500% higher than ordered materials.*

Worse, shortages of these small items stalled production. A 0.50 Riyal sleeve could stop a fitting worth 500 Riyals.

We placed bulk orders for all frequently-short items, even airlifting some for emergencies. Instruction was issued for prior approval by me before purchase of any item using petty cash. This single instruction saved money, avoided delays, and protected product quality. The unseen cost drivers were finally brought to light.

Change #29: Disciplinary Action- A Necessary Storm

Al-Babtain Group, in general, does not follow a hire-and-fire policy, and it is common to find employees with over 25 years of service at all levels. Such long service naturally breeds loyalty and a strong sense of ownership, something that cannot be achieved by any other means.

However, three months into the job, I had to make a tough decision regarding an erring employee. He was habitually late by hours, which severely impacted the planning function. Despite repeated verbal reminders, his behaviour continued.

In consultation with higher authorities, we followed the appropriate procedures as per Saudi Labour Laws to correct the situation. All warnings were ignored for reasons unknown. At the next offence, he was relieved from the service of ALCO. It was a rare action within the group.

Because all procedures were followed and documented, there was no room for complaints, although there were comments from many. The management supported the decision fully. This incident set the tone for the rest of my tenure there.

Key Learnings:

1. An unexpected bonus is pure joy. Recognition satisfies deeper than money.
2. Sunlight is nature's most powerful workforce energiser.
3. Petty cash purchases silently drain profitability; ignoring them is costly.
4. Timely disciplinary action—even when emotionally difficult—creates clarity, respect, and a ripple effect across the organisation.

Reflections:

November delivered another 5 million SR month, our second consecutive one. Confidence soared. Bonus lifted morale. Sunlit skylights lifted spirits. The factory ran in two shifts, tea flowed generously, and discipline strengthened.

Daily reports showed improving numbers, backlog shrinking, deliveries climbing, new orders arriving steadily. Something remarkable was happening at ALCO.

For the first time, we sensed a possibility. We could close the year at par with last year's 40 million SR. We set an ambitious target of SR 5.5 million for December.

The ALCO that existed in August had disappeared. A new ALCO was rising - brighter, sharper, more united, and hungry for success.

7

The Month of Discipline and Ambition

Month 5 – December 2009

With back-to-back 5 million SR delivery months, ALCO was buzzing with activity. The Production Bonus had energized the floor. Purchase, Sales, and Accounts were now packed with ALCO-related work. Momentum was flowing in our favour and we needed to keep pushing.

For December, we set a simple, aggressive target:

"Dispatch SR 200,000 worth of material every single day".

If anything fell short, supervisors were permitted to use parts from available stock. The maintenance team, R&D staff, even drivers, everyone stepped into production. Job rotation has now become a culture not just a policy.

Change #30: Freeze the Production Plan

Frequent changes in daily schedules often from Sales or sister companies were disrupting production plans. Open work orders were stopped midway, WIP piled up, and stores were thrown into chaos.Expeditors barged in, demanded items urgently, and stayed back until it was done. It was chaotic, frustrating, and unsustainable.

When verbal reminders didn't work, wrote formally to all concerned Heads:

New Rules for the Monthly Plan:

1. Next month's production plan shall be finalized by PPC and shared by the 25th for acceptance or revision by 27th.
2. Only 2 changes allowed during the following month .
3. Any change must come in writing, from the concerned Manager to the Operations Manager.

Supervisors and engineers were instructed to follow instruction strictly and expeditors were to be shown a copy of the instruction and seek my permission. The effect was immediate, plans stabilized, visit of expeditors stopped and the factory did not lose its momentum

Change #31: Vacation is to Be Availed, Not Accumulated

A disturbing pattern came to light: Many employees had not taken leave for years. One hadn't gone home for eight years.

This created two problems:

1. declining health,
2. people beginning to feel indispensable

But depending on one single employee is a hidden risk to the company.

We worked with HR to prepare an aging report. After discussion, a circular was issued to all department heads. I had, by now become a fan of ageing reports!!

"Submit the planned vacation dates of all employees for the next six months. Leave is meant to be used, not postponed".

Later, this became a Group-wide policy, with limits on leave accumulation. Sometimes the best way to show care is to insist that people rest. Also,it removed the feeling of indispensability amongst employees.

Change #32: Decision to Pursue ISO 14001 & OHSAS 18001 Certification

By year-end, Management announced that all factories would pursue certification for **ISO 14001 (Environmental Management)** and **OHSAS 18001 (Occupational Health & Safety).**

The timeline: Audit by mid-2010. Responsibility: Factory heads

Just like the penalty notice in August, this too felt like a blessing disguised as pressure. These certifications meant higher standards of:

1. safety
2. housekeeping
3. environmental compliance
4. structural discipline

Exactly what ALCO needed.

Change #33: Buying a Drivable Floor-Cleaning Machine

With the decision to go for a new certification, the focus shifted to housekeeping. Cleaning the floor manually was time-consuming and usually got delayed until almost mid-day. The cleaner would attend to other tasks first and only then begin cleaning the floor. To solve this, we decided to purchase a battery-operated drivable floor cleaner, a standard model available in the market.

With this machine, the entire factory floor could be cleaned in less than one hour . Employees were instructed to keep the passages free for smooth cleaning. A designated parking space and charging point were arranged for the machine, and the key was kept with the despatch in-charge. The cleaner's first task every morning was to clean the floor, and by 7:30 a.m., the entire factory was spick and span.

Change #34: Farewells That End with Happiness

One afternoon, a staff member approached me with a collection request. A long-serving employee was leaving. His colleagues wanted to buy him a gift with collected money. This surprised me. Farewell should be a company's gratitude not a burden on colleagues. I stopped the collection immediately and implemented a new system:

1. ALCO would host the farewell in the dining room.
2. A fixed budget would be allotted for the gift from company.
3. The employee could choose the gift; if the cost exceeded , he bore the difference.
4. Pastries and soft drinks were borne by the company.

This became a heartfelt tradition at ALCO. Everyone left with dignity, respect, and smiles. Even when I left, they honoured me the same way and that remains one of my cherished memories.

Change #35: Visitor Badges-Stopping Hidden Disruptions

One Thursday, I visited office to finish some urgent work. A stranger was sitting in the meeting room with employees lining up to meet him.

After enquiring with security, I learned that he was from a bank and was offering salary-based loans. He visits regularly on Thursday and had built a large customer base. All documentation was done inside our office, which was affecting production and was certainly not appropriate. This was unacceptable and was affecting productivity.

I called him to my office and advised him to visit our accommodation after office hours in the future. I also instructed the security team not to allow such visitors inside the premises. Then we implemented a strict system:

1. Visitor Badge
2. Visitor Book

3. Mandatory Helmet
4. ID or License in exchange for the badge

Security was instructed that every visitor including drivers coming to collect goods must be issued a badge in exchange for an ID card or driving licence. The visit details had to be recorded in the Visitor Book. Many ex-employees, service providers, and friends were visiting ALCO for personal purposes. Although some visitors objected initially, the security was strict, and soon the system became the norm.

We even discovered that the labour supplier contractor was distributing salaries inside our factory, causing disruption to production. This practice was also stopped. Three to four such visits every month by service providers resulted in significant productivity loss:

1. **Number of workers:** 50 (Company)
2. **Time lost per visit**: 1 hour
3. **Frequency per month**: 4
4. **Total time lost**: 200 hours and that is equivalent to one month of labour.

Sometimes simple discipline saves weeks of productivity.

Change #36: The Hissing Sound - A Silent Power Drain

Maintenance was repairing a pneumatic tool on the shop floor and I observed it at close quarters. Heard a hissing noise from a nearby table, then another, and another, all air leaks from the compressed air lines. A walkthrough revealed over 50 leakage points. Air loss meant:

1. compressors running longer,
2. higher electricity bills,
3. reduced tool efficiency.

We fixed every leak with :

1. better washers
2. simpler routing
3. fewer bends
4. stronger joints

Within ten days, the "hissing orchestra" disappeared. The compressor ran less, saving huge amounts of energy. Though we didn't measure ALCO's exact savings, later applying the same principle in a matchbox factory in Tamil Nadu we saved:

- 125 units/day → 43,750 units/year
- At INR16/unit → INR 7,00,000 saved annually

Change #37: Appraisals and the Forced Distribution Challenge

By mid-December, HR sent the appraisal format for increment with instruction to follow the forced distribution system championed by GE. Under this system, the bottom 10% of employees received no increment, while the remaining 90% received a raise based on ranking. The bottom 10% would then be relieved from service.

However, the system had a major flaw in Saudi Arabian context. Replacing the bottom 10% was not feasible in Saudi Arabia due to visa limitations, and hiring nationals was not easy. Moreover, even the 90% who received increments would not truly enjoy their raise, as their colleagues in the bottom 10% with whom they shared strong camaraderie received nothing.

Met my boss and shared my concerns, explaining that such a system was not suitable as replacement of the bottom tier was not possible. I requested an exemption for ALCO and asked for permission to distribute the increment among all employees, while keeping the total allocated amount unchanged.

Initially, HR resisted the proposal. However, given the strong performance in October and November, my boss supported the idea after accepting the logic. This resulted in a policy change . Everyone received a raise within the same total budget. A long-standing policy shifted because logic prevailed over tradition.

Change #38: The Audacious 2010 Budget

As 2010 was approaching, it was Budget time. The factory's budget was based on the Sales Forecast, as that was the starting point for all planning. Based on the deliveries of the last three months, I requested the Sales Department to increase the forecast by 50% over the previous year. They raised it by 25%, instead of the usual 10%. This increase was important to avoid seeking special permission later for purchases exceeding the approved budget; another good practice followed at Babtain.

Although my boss was initially sceptical, he eventually nodded his approval, and we budgeted for a revenue of SR 50 million. Ambitious? Yes. Impossible? Not anymore. ALCO had changed mindsets and ambition had become a habit.

Key Learnings:

1. Traditions must be supported by Logic.
2. Practises of one country may not be applicable to another .
3. Aim high-only then do you discover how high you can actually climb.

Reflections:

December closed with yet another SR 5 million plus delivery. Three months earlier, nobody would have believed this possible.

ALCO matched the previous year's turnover, something unimaginable in September.

The factory was cleaner, brighter, more organised, and far more disciplined. Resistance to change had faded because people could see the results.

The low profits of early 2009, the penalty, and the push for certifications all turned out to be blessings in disguise.

8

The Quiet Work of Building Strength

Month 6 – January 2010

The New Year began with a lot of promise and hope. We started the year with a sumptuous lunch for all employees, a simple gesture that set the tone for the months ahead. We closed 2009 slightly above the 2008 figures, and although the bottom-line had marginally improved, a bottom line of just 4% was not very encouraging. But it brought something more important: relief. The fear of closure, a shadow that hovered over ALCO for months was finally gone.

We aimed to despatch goods worth over SR 5 million every month, and the order backlog was improving. The two certifications and achieving SR 5 million in monthly deliveries became our key focus areas, and everyone was requested to contribute to these objectives.

Change #39: The Cost-Reduction Project - A Collective Promise

Management approved the increment for 2010, but with a caveat: sincere efforts had to be made to reduce costs. This instruction was given to all group managers, as profitability had declined in the two years following the 2008 recession. The order book had also reduced. A similar cost-reduction initiative had been carried out in 1999–2000 when project volumes were low and pricing was under pressure.

One of the senior managers of the group was assigned the responsibility of coordinating this project. At ALCO, a team was formed comprising a design engineer, a planning engineer, and a production engineer to identify after cost-reduction opportunities at least enough to offset the additional burden created by the increment. A notice was put up inviting everyone to participate. The team was given a week to identify potential opportunities and quantify the savings.

They came up with around ten ideas across various areas, and this initiative soon evolved into an ongoing project. This was another blessing in our turnaround effort, as cost reduction now became an official priority. The message landed: this was our company, and every rupee saved belonged to our future.

Change #40: Reorganising Electrical Assembly - Traceability Equals Trust

The electrical assembly section had begun to choke the flow. Around 25 people handled control gear assembly from end to end, one person building the whole , another testing, and the same parts moving haphazardly until a failure surfaced. Valuable Time was wasted waiting for testing or moving the parts .

We studied the flow , rearranged the tables and split the work into clear roles: mechanical fitters, electricians, helpers and testers . ID stickers and traceability were introduced so every unit could be back-tracked to the person who made it. If a unit failed in testing, it was returned to the responsible station for correction. Old tools were replaced where needed and other low cost modernisation was introduced to speed up the process .

The result was profound: faster throughput, fewer reworks, and a team that began to trust numbers and one another. Productivity rose because the work had been decanted into smaller, accountable steps and people felt the dignity of mastery rather than the burden of blame. A record was maintained for completed Control gear assemblies further improving output . A scoreboard does wonders .

Change #41: Certification - A Punch List and a Promise

ISO 14001 and OHSAS 18001 audits loomed . The consultant's first visit in January produced a punch list of over 100 items. It was tempting to delay; to say we'd prepare "later." But ALCO decided to take the punch list head-on.

At lunchtime the next day I gathered everyone and spoke plainly: this certification matters, for our business and for our safety. We assigned responsibility to Production Engineers for shop-floor items, Maintenance Head for stores, lab and office. Each morning I'd receive an updated list and slowly the list became smaller . In two weeks, wiring was dressed, broken parts were fixed, loose wires anchored , tools were made safe, and the shop floor looked like a place that cared for its people. People often rise when they feel trusted, this was one such moment.

Change #42: Resetting Stores - Think Vertical, Not Just Horizontal

A lot of material had moved out of the stores, and the space was no longer as congested as before. We needed additional areas because production activities had increased, and as per the initial report to management, the store was to be relocated near the gate to minimise internal movement .

Although the Stores Manager was initially reluctant to reduce the store size, after a couple of meetings and exchanging ideas, he agreed to eliminate the last two racks so that we could save 5 meters of floor space by utilising the Z-axis more effectively. Many pallets and cartons had only 50% occupancy, so we decided to store more than one item in a pallet or carton with proper labelling.

Within a week, we were able to reduce the store area by removing the last two columns while adding one more level to the existing racks.

1. **Floor area saved:** 16%
2. **Storage space increased:** 25%

The removed purlins were reused to create the new levels in the remaining racks.

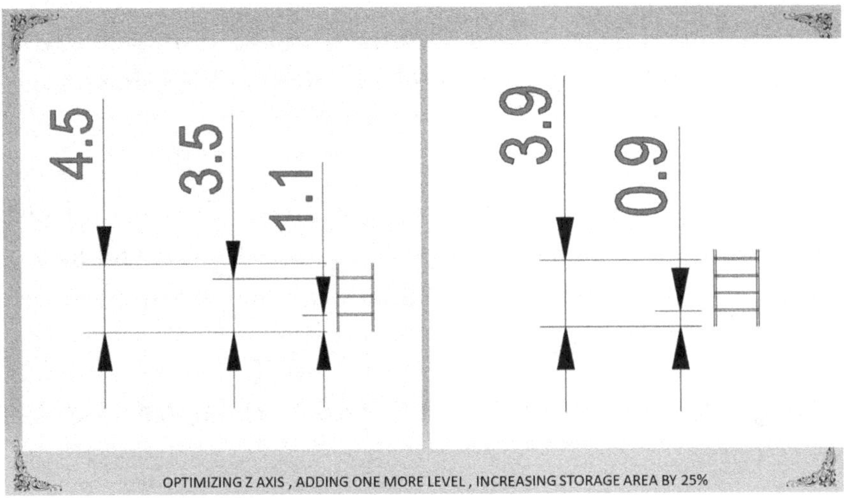

Figure 3: Optimizing Z axis, adding one more level & increasing storage area by 25%

Change #43: Use Stock with Modification – Innovate

As deliveries increased, shortages also began to rise. Packing cartons and gaskets became critical, and ordering new supplies required both quantity and time. While the exact required items may be short, other sizes were available in stock. Advised the Design team to check whether these available sizes could be modified for use without compromising quality or purpose. PPC was instructed to raise a formal request with a copy to QC, and tests were conducted before final approval.

This study proved to be a major boost, as many items could indeed be used with simple modifications. Production continued without interruption, and emergency purchases were avoided. One example that comes to mind is the 6×4 gasket, which was short but 6x12 gasket was available .All that was needed was a jig and fixture to cut the larger gasket into three perfect pieces, something the supervisor developed immediately. IP tests were conducted using the modified part and the luminaire was found satisfactory.

Similarly, when the 500×800×600 carton was short, a 1000×850×600 carton was used to pack two units together , a small packing piece deployed to fill the gap. As they say, *"Necessity is the mother of invention."*

In addition to reducing inventory, this approach freed up storage space and nurtured a culture of finding practical alternatives.

Change #44: Closing Half the Gate - Reclaiming Space

During a routine review of the store layout, noticed that the main passage inside the store was 6 meters wide, far more than what our operations required. This was due to the width of the two halves of the gate which was 3 m each . Since a width of just 3 meters was sufficient for the safe movement of vehicles, we made a strategic decision to permanently close one half of the gate.

This simple shift unlocked three meters of additional floor space, which we immediately converted into productive storage area by adding a new row of racks creating 120 sq. m of additional storage capacity. We applied the same approach in the FG store, further expanding our usable space and improving material flow.

To ensure that this improvement remained sustainable, I instituted a monthly review of the stores between the 20th and 25th and advised the Planning Department to minimize material-issue requests after the

20th. This brought discipline, free time , and far better planning into the system.

Impact:

1. **Floor space saved:** 120 sq. m (3 m × 40 m)
2. **Storage space increased**: 120 sq. m (8 columns × 5 levels × 3)

A small but decisive action closing half a gate created room for efficiency, strengthened operational discipline, and turned unused space into a productive asset. The racks removed earlier found meaningful new purpose, completing the cycle of smart resource utilization.

Change #45: Specify Rejection Criteria - End the Tug-of-War with QC

One of the recurring points of conflict between Production and QC was the lack of clarity on what was considered unacceptable. After completing a product, QC often rejected it for minor issues such as small grease marks, tiny scratches, or faint lines.

These frequent hold-ups were affecting output and relationship . Requested QC to formally define the rejection criteria. While acceptance criteria were clearly documented and known , rejection criteria were not. After referring to relevant standards, QC prepared clear rejection limits, and Production was instructed to follow the new guidelines.

The guidelines were displayed prominently across the shop floor to eliminate ambiguity. This transparency reduced resentment, aligned both departments, and restored flow in production.

Change #46: Publishing the Rationale for Increments - Transparency Heals

Increments were announced in the last week of January, and suddenly many employees felt undervalued. With the management's permission, we published the complete rationale behind the increments and clarified how no one had been left out. This helped employees understand that ALCO had, in fact cared for all its employees and the available cake was shared by all.

This transparent explanation was a first in the Group and it immediately restored trust, reduced misunderstandings, and strengthened morale.

Key Learnings:

1. Traceability reduces rejections and increases accountability.
2. Stores are elastic; they expand or contract based on our creativity.
3. A 3-meter passage is more than sufficient for vehicle movement, given that the maximum vehicle width is only about 2.2 meters.
4. Using the Z axis effectively relieves pressure on the X and Y axis.

Reflections:

January was not loud. It was not dramatic. It was not glamorous.

It was disciplined work: creating space, clearing bottlenecks, enforcing standards, improving processes, and preparing for certification.

We closed January above SR 4 million, and set February's target at 4 million again.

With cleaner stores, better traceability, and a shrinking punch list, ALCO was structurally stronger ,ready for deeper cost reduction, especially in materials.January laid the foundation for long-term strength.

Implementation Record:

Sr. No.	Date	Reference change #	Reduce consumption of	Improve Output of	Value

9

The Month of Smart Savings

Month 7 – February 2010

February arrived with clarity!

A clarity that efficiency is not just about numbers but about understanding people, processes, and possibilities. What began as routine operational reviews turned into a month of profound transformation.

Change #47: Bulk Ordering with Heart and Foresight

For years, ALCO ordered materials every month, and every time ,the price was re-negotiated. Prices shifted like desert sands : raw material hikes, freight fluctuations, currency swings, everything pushed costs upward. One component stood out: aluminium castings which ALCO imports in big numbers.

Instead of continuing the cycle, we decided to do something simple yet rarely done, visit the supplier, sit with them, and understand their struggle. To our surprise, they were mirroring our chaos. They ordered aluminium only after receiving our orders. They were dealing with the same uncertainties we were battling.

When two teams sat across the table, not as buyer and seller but as partners, the solution emerged:

The solution: Bulk ordering with staggered delivery.

This allowed them to place firm orders for aluminium ingots in advance, secure stable pricing, and pass on a discount to us. We agreed to confirm exact items 45 days ahead, quantity good enough for a full 40-ft container.

Returning to the factory, we drafted a one-year requirement chart and placed the bulk order. Overnight, the endless price negotiations disappeared. Encouraged by this, we extended the model to all major suppliers: electrical components, wires, and more. Copper prices was equally truant . Suppliers appreciated our trust and reciprocated with better service and terms.

Savings: Considerable savings as most suppliers gave us a discount above 5%. But more importantly, we built relationships based on trust, not transactions.

Change #48: The Paint that Flaked—and the Lesson that Shined

One morning, an entire lot of luminaires was rejected due to paint flaking. Coating thickness had crossed 80 microns, double the required 40. It was wasteful and expensive. This rejection became an opportunity.

During a deep dive with Production, Maintenance, Design and QC, we realised something subtle yet powerful: The specification spoke of 40 microns, but it didn't define minimum or average. Armed with insights from the Pole & Tower factory's experience in galvanizing control, we revised our entire approach:

- 40 microns as the average coating thickness
- A sample check for every 10th piece
- Regular maintenance of spray nozzles
- Clear instructions in PPC work orders
- Alerts for thickness above 60 microns

Within a week, paint consumption dropped by 20%. Another major variable cost was brought under control , not by force, but by understanding. With savings from Aluminium, Copper and paint, profits took a different dimension .

Change #49: The Showroom That Told Our Story

ALCO manufactures about 55 models of luminaires, ranging from 70 watts to 2000 watts. Customers and end clients from various municipalities often visited the factory with the Sales team to evaluate and approve models. Many a times, the meeting table was used to display the proposed fittings, but without illumination, customers could neither appreciate the product nor see its lighting effect. We were hiding our strengths. So, it was decided to build something special: a showroom that told the story of our craftsmanship.

Old display stands from past exhibitions were brought back, modified, wired , repainted, and put to good use . Within a week, the display centre was ready, showcasing nearly 25 types of fittings, each with a nameplate and salient features. Most of the models were organised as a series to represent different wattages clearly. And ,they could be switched on .

When customers walked in, something magical happened. After seeing the products they experienced them. They saw light, design, precision, ease of operation. They saw the passion behind our work.

This initiative led to many new orders, as customers finally became aware of the full range of luminaires and Floodlights ALCO produced. Visitors who arrived during lunch hours were entertained with lunch, reinforcing our culture of hospitality.

Key Learnings:

1. Variable cost can be reduced either by lowering consumption or securing better procurement terms or better by doing both .
2. Bulk ordering with staggered delivery reduces headaches and builds trust, and stability.

3. A product showroom is not just a display; it is a bridge between what we create and what the world needs to see.

And behind all these improvements lies one truth:

When we respect people, understand processes, and show our strengths with pride, progress becomes inevitable.

Reflections:

February was the month we realised how strongly variable costs drive profitability, and how simple but powerful changes can reshape our entire economics:

- Bulk ordering saved millions in material cost over the year
- Paint thickness control cut consumption by 20%
- The new showroom helped win more orders
- Budget is again a guideline . Improve it for better results

February ended with deliveries above 3 million and as one staff put it, February has only 28 days !

10

The Month of Innovation and Incentives

Month 8 – March 2010

March 2010 arrived with a question that echoed across the factory floor:

"Can we bring back the fire of last quarter of 2009?"

The first two months of the year had been slow. Deliveries didn't meet expectations, and the energy that once fuelled our extraordinary momentum seemed to fade. But sometimes, it takes one spark to light a dormant furnace.

This month, that spark came in many forms, an incentive, a specification review, a revived machine, and even a home-made lift. March became the month where the factory rediscovered its heartbeat.

Change #50: Quarterly Incentive Linked to Despatch:

Turning Performance into Motivation. To restore the rhythm of high dispatches, achieved in 2009, proposed a quarterly incentive scheme to the management, something transparent, predictable and merit-based. Unlike the earlier bonus, this was linked to deliveries, above a certain volume. Management agreed. The incentive structure was similar to the October bonus, but now it was tied directly to dispatch performance. The idea was simple:

- Fittings up to 400W → One category
- Fittings above 400W → Second category
- Accessories and panel boards → Third category
- Achieve targets monthly → get paid for the month but quarterly

You could earn incentive for one month, two months, or all three months of the quarter depending on achievement. The scheme was published and everybody could know why they got or did not get .This was first-of-its-kind in the entire group. Soon, other group of factories began copying the model. The most beautiful shift happened on the shop floor. Production began asking Planning:

"What should we produce today?"

Planning began asking Sales:

"Where is the release order? What's the priority?"

Material planners started chasing Purchase:

"We need this material today, not tomorrow."

The incentive linked every department like a perfectly engineered chain. Targets and achievements were displayed for all to see. Every person knew what to aim for, what to finish, what mattered. By the end of the quarter, employees had earned incentive for two months . The smiles spoke louder than numbers.

Change #51: Rethinking the Inside Paint

Success in reducing paint consumption in February encouraged us to challenge another long-followed but never questioned practice. Should the inner surface of Luminaires get painted to 40 microns? Every luminaire was being painted inside and outside to minimum 40 microns. But the inner surface:

- was not exposed to atmosphere
- was enclosed (most fittings were IP65 or above)

- had no mention in the specification

After detailed discussions with QC and Design, we made a bold decision: Not to paint the inner surface and accept whatever small coating naturally sticks during the process. The result:

- **First reduction**: 100 kg → 80 kg (20%)
- **Second reduction**: 80 kg → 40 kg (50%)

Total reduction: 60% paint consumption in just two months. Quality remained intact. This was a breakthrough. Variable cost reduction unlocked by simple logic. Not a single complaint came until the day I left. This is what happens when we stop assuming.

Upgrading & Modernisation

When Innovation is born from Dust, Scrap, and Imagination. Our certification work was progressing well. Punch list had almost disappeared . It was time to modernize the systems that were stuck in the past. Many manual tasks had to evolve. And most thrilling of all, we decided to build machines ourselves as we were an engineering unit.

Change #52: The Wire Cutting Machine and others

Wire cutting was done laboriously by hand and it was disorganised. Earlier there was a mechanised wire cutting machine but discontinued due to some spares shortage .Decided to revive and upgrade it. The technician who developed it was available and he got his baby ready in a week .Now, the operator simply fed wire coils and set the lengths while the machine did the rest. A counter was also fixed to show the count.

Daily wire requirements were delivered with precision and zero wastage. Many such manual tasks were slowly converted into mechanised operations and each one added a drop of efficiency to the ocean of productivity.

Change #53: The Home-Made Lift

Our R&D department was on the ground floor while Offices were on the first . A steel stairway connected the two. Customers frequently visited R&D, which also housed mould-making facilities. But climbing the narrow steel staircase was inconvenient and tiresome. So, we decided to build our own in-house lift. Ye , a lift. Our product development engineer led the project with great passion, and we carried out the following series of tasks:

1. A lift house with aluminium frame and transparent walls of polycarbonate sheets was built in-house to fit the available space,
2. A 660 kg winch from our sister Factory which make High mast was used to raise and lower the housing.
3. Sensors and controls were added
4. Emergency switches installed.

Soon, a fully operational, beautiful in-house lift stood where an old staircase once did. Visitors loved it. Employees were proud of it. It became the symbol of what ALCO was becoming as a factory, where ideas turned into reality.

Change #54: The Home-Made Dust Extraction System

The grinding and finishing section were always covered with aluminium dust. Every two hours, someone had to manually clean the area. This wasn't sustainable. So, we built our own dust extraction system entirely in-house. My earlier experience in designing and marketing of Air Pollution control equipment and systems for steel and cement factories became helpful. Materials used:

- A discarded conical pole (from Pole Factory) was used as a Cyclone !
- A discarded old centrifugal fan was revived

- A 2 HP motor, available in house was used as the drive
- 2 inch and half an inch Pipes from scrap served as the ducting
- Rubber balls used in fancy key chains was bought for just SR 1 each to act as a damper to control the suction points

We designed a cyclone system with 8 suction points connected to a central line and connectable to the two flexible hoses .Any dust within a radius of 20 m could be sucked. A gate valve below the Cyclone maintained the pressure .It was opened every one hour to collect the dust accumulated at the bottom of the cyclone. The shop floor transformed : Clean. Clear. Healthy. All at a cost of SR 8 (US $ 2.2/). Yes, a working dust extraction system for less than $ 2.2.

Key Learnings:

1. Financial reward is a great motivator.
2. Innovating and finding solutions in-house is more rewarding and enjoyable than simply purchasing them.
3. When change becomes a routine, resistance disappears.

Reflections:

It was another good month for reducing variable costs and manual labour. The quarterly incentive proved to be a great motivator for achieving more. The first quarter ended with strong dispatch performance, making employees eligible for two months' incentive. Scrap value realised increased as output grew. Apart from the lunch programs, we started giving special bonuses to employees who contributed to the development work. The maintenance team was rewarded regularly as they were responsible for the majority of the changes.

The good news was that other factories in the group also started offering production incentives, and many employees from those factories called to thank me. People were now dreaming of getting 13 months' salary in a year!

11

The Month Bottlenecks Broke and Space Expanded

Month 9 –April 2010

The factory was now dispatching almost 5 million SR every month and the once-impossible had become routine. Orders flowed steadily. The quarterly incentive had lifted morale. Despatching felt like it was on auto-pilot.

Yet, beneath the surface, one truth remained: *A factory grows only when its bottlenecks shrink.*

And in April, we went after two of the biggest bottlenecks ALCO had carried for years: Painting and Storage area .

Change #55: Painting Line Overhaul

Our automatic electrostatic painting line, an imported system with conveyors and 120 hangers was supposed to be our pride. But in reality, it had become our biggest pain and bottleneck. The paint wasn't curing. QC was rejecting entire lots. Production halted frequently. The oven wasn't generating enough heat. Every shutdown delayed delivery.

We had patched it too many times. Now it was time to fix it forever. We announced a 10-day shutdown, a bold decision, but a necessary one. Planned orders were prepared in advance so that the line could be freed for the overhaul.

The Discovery That Shocked Us All

Maintenance had touched all parts of the oven and painting line except the two centrifugal fans. Technicians from the original manufacturer had not visited for ages. Under my assurance, the maintenance team finally opened the first fan. What we saw left us speechless.

The impeller of the fan and the casing were solidly packed with hardened paint. Only 10% of space was free. The root cause was the water in the desert cooler placed near the painters for comfort . The water and paint mix deposited inside the fan, and the build-up turned rock solid over the years

For two straight days, the team chipped away the hardened mass until the metal appeared again. We cleaned it, balanced the impeller and tested it.No one could stand close, it was throwing air with unbelievable force, like the machine had come alive after years of suffocation. We re-installed it. And in 20 minutes, the oven reached 240°C effortlessly. The line was reborn.

A Complete Transformation

- We replaced the rusted steel pipes and nozzles with PVC.
- Stopped leaks.
- Inside walls was cladded with SS sheets
- Rebuilt the drain pit.
- Repainted the entire line.

In 15 days, the painting line looked, and performed like a brand-new system. **And the results?**

- Working days increased from 20 to 25.
- Overall painting output jumped by over **25%**.

A bottleneck and uncertainty that had haunted us for years disappeared in two weeks of focused teamwork.

Change #56: The Mosque Modification

Summer had started and one afternoon, a few employees approached me and said: *"Sir, the mosque AC is not working well. Can we repair it?"* In Saudi Arabia, every workplace has a prayer hall. It is not just a room; it is a sacred space. A place where people recharge spiritually and emotionally. It deserved a makeover. I visited the mosque myself and saw its condition. That same day, we arranged:

- Two new split A/c's of 1.5 tons with timer. One person was given the responsibility to set the timer to switch on half an hour before the next prayer.
- Pedestal fans

Over the weekend:

- Old window AC openings were closed
- Walls repainted
- Carpets replaced
- Ablution area reset and retiled
- Shoe rack built

The following week, the QC Manager, an Egyptian gentleman, visited me after offering his prayers. His eyes reflected genuine gratitude. He thanked me profusely.

Soon, visitors from other plants also began using the mosque. Cleaning schedules were set before and after prayers. The mosque became a place of peace. When you respect what your people respect, the reward comes from above.

Change #57: Create space out of thin air

With 2–3 containers of castings arriving at a time, our racks overflowed instantly. Only one carton could fit on each rack, creating a severe space crunch that made movement difficult. As a result, production suffered.

We needed storage space but building extensions was not possible and new warehouses was expensive. So ,we were compelled to find additional space and the search started. The focus was on finding free space in the shop floor and store but we had already used every nook and corner .

The factory was built on steel columns spaced six meters apart and there was over 60 such columns around the factory . The ceiling was about 7m high at the sides and about 9 m height in the centre

The Breakthrough

It became a regular subject of discussion amongst us whenever we met and during one such shopfloor meets , the idea of creating another shop floor emerged . Two level beds were common in bachelor accommodation and someone suggested it. (Regret ,I don't remember who suggested). Bingo !!

The idea:

Build platforms of 4 m width at 3m height. Use the building columns (I Beams) as support on one side. So, two columns can hold one 40 feet container load. Store all material only on pallets. Use hand pulled trolley for moving material on platform and forklift to raise. All Safety precautions to be taken, create Emergency exits.

In a day the idea had crystallised into a two-tier structure, with the potential of generating:

380m (perimeter of building) x 4m (width of platform) x 2(tiers) =3040 sq. m (32,710 sq. ft.)of floor area

3040sq.m x 4mheight = 2160 cu. m (131,000 sq. ft) considering stacking height of 2m.

Capable to house to approximately 250 nos 40 feet container load.

The Space constraint just evaporated.

The Tower Factory designers created the structural designs , and within two weeks, two platforms of 6m length each were built, capable to house 4 nos. 40 feet container loads . The columns near the receiving gate were selected to reduce the distance travelled from unloading to store. Al Babtain , being a major Steel High masts and Tower manufacturer ,all material could be arranged from our sister factories and the maintenance team did the construction.

Now unloading and storing a full container load could be accomplished in less than half an hour by one forklift and one assistant on the platform . Earlier it took up to two hours by two forklifts after a lot of preparatory work . Even the truck drivers were stunned as they were released in a jiffy. The platforms released more area for production and eased the strain on the existing stores.

Group thinking saved time, money, and operational headaches and this change proved it. In course of time most columns in the building became support for the platforms creating another two shop floors.

Later, as a consultant this idea was shared and adopted by many companies successfully .This is a universal solution for space constraint. Instead of hiring new space, build platforms and save on space , energy consumed, maintenance cost and man hours !!!!!

Change #58: Reducing Chemical Store Size

The chemical store , a separate covered area inside the Stores was 12m × 6m in size , fully air-conditioned with its own passage of 3mx 4m apart from two emergency exits . But during summer, temperatures inside was higher than the permitted. The store requested two more AC units. Instead of approving the unit , we visited the store.

Inside, we saw materials that didn't need cooling at all, even products used in the foundry were there . Assigned the Store Head , Design and QC to list only items requiring controlled temperature. The result?

- The store needed only 6m × 6m space with racks

- The separate passage could be avoided if entrance from the main passage is opened
- One emergency door was enough and the other pathway was put to good use
- The existing AC units were sufficient
- Saved 48 sq. m of valuable space. (6x6 +3x4).

Sometimes, Solution don't need money. They just need fresh eyes.

Key Learnings:

1. Rewards must be given quickly to maximise their motivational impact.
2. Eliminate bottlenecks because they limit everything.
3. Wonders happen when people start working not just with hands, but with mind and heart.

Reflections:
April was a month of breaking bottlenecks and reclaiming space.

- The painting line, ALCO's biggest constraint was eliminated .
- Storage space , another bottleneck vanished .
- Mosque upliftment boosted morale
- Deliveries touched 5 million SR again, keeping the spirit alive

Employees earned their bonuses, and the factory felt unstoppable. But the best part? Everything was achieved in-house, with ingenuity and teamwork not capital expenditure.

ALCO was learning that when people believe in the goal, miracles become habitual.

Implementation Record:

Sr. No.	Date	Reference change #	Reduce consump-tion of	Improve Output of	Value

12

The Month of Flow, Speed, and Invisible Savings

Month 10 – May 2010

By the time May arrived, ALCO felt and was different. Deliveries had become smooth. Target now felt like milestones on a highway and we were driving on it confidently. Dispatching 5 million SR without additional manpower, without new machines, without new budgets was routine now.

The factory had begun to run like a well-tuned engine. Momentum was real. Confidence was growing. ALCO was running almost on autopilot. And in May, our focus narrowed to enhancing the flow of work, its speed, visibility and communication.

Change #59: The Real-Time Packing Report

Packing was the last step before despatch and was recorded manually on a register, updated by the packing head. Delays, errors, and information gaps were common.

As IT was booming, we tried it in packing section . IT head took up the challenge . Placed a desktop right at the packing point. Every hour or on completing a batch the packing section head entered what was packed. The production engineer pre-set the table with model and quantity, making the job as simple as typing the finished quantity. The screen was visible to all concerned and without leaving the seat we could know what was packed up to the last hour. Suddenly, the whole factory could see what was happening in real time.

- Weekends and after-hours became just as productive as day shifts.
- Guests and visitors could witness the IT revolution in our packing section.

The IT Head had done a brilliant job. But more importantly the factory had discovered the power of real-time information.

Change #60: Moving the IP Lab

With the new display centre, the time spent by visitors in ALCO increased. We often took them to see the Ingress Protection (IP) lab, which was located inside the factory. This lab tested light fittings for protection against both water and dust and was certified to conduct tests up to IP67. Apart from IP testing, electrical and mechanical tests were also conducted for components and fitting making the lab a valuable intellectual asset. Most visitors were keen to see it.

Given the high level of interest, we decided to relocate the IP lab to the main building, directly opposite the display centre. A large area was set aside for this purpose, and within about ten days, the entire setup was transferred. With improved lighting, a dedicated viewing area, and personal protective equipment (PPE) kits, the new IP lab looked like a scene from a science-fiction movie.

Change #61: Setting Right, the Fouling Cable Trays

Store modification had become a monthly ritual. Every month we found space. Every month we reclaimed something lost. This time it was from the fouling cable trays.

We found trays positioned poorly, fouling and wasting a full foot of space along a 50-meter length. By simply correcting the alignment, we recovered 50 meters × 1 feet of space = 15 sq.m

Not a huge saving but these small recoveries added up space inside the factory. In a factory like ALCO, every corner and every inch matters and we proved it with this change.

Change #62: Reducing Material Travel Distance

This was one of the changes closest to my heart because the problem was observed every single day from my office window.

Stores has two gates :

- One for outside access ,permitting small vehicles inside
- One for inside access , issuing material into the factory

"Why only two gates ? " was my first question to Stores Head.

Because, it is a policy decision and practised in all factories. Also, Stores, as a policy reported to the Top management, not Factory Head.

The issuing gate was in the first bay at 40 m from the back wall . But the machines needing material were in the second or third bay, throughout the 120m length of the factory.

The forklift had to travel at times 150 meters, one way, disturbing every aisle, every human, every operation to deliver the material for processing. It happened at least 25- 30 times a day. That meant:

- **Average of 6 km** of forklift travel per day @ 100m one way
- **156 km** per month

All inside the factory. All efforts and expenses adding No value. In discussion with Stores and Top Management, it was permitted to open more gates but with more vigil. We revised the entire storing plan. Material was placed in aisles inside the store but closer to the machines.

Travel distance dropped dramatically from 150 meters to even 10 meters in some cases. The average distance travelled dropped to 25 m

Now:

- Forklift travel reduced from **156 km → 39 km**
- **117 km saved every month**
- Huge savings in time, tyres, power, battery, and manpower
- Deliveries became lightning fast

This single improvement increased speed, and productivity across the factory. Forklift drivers were free for other tasks!

Change #63: Bridging the Racks

After opening new gates, a technician came up with a brilliant idea:

"Sir, why not bridge the racks above 2.5 meters? Forklifts travel only up to 2 meters. The space above is empty."

The idea was gold.

Using specially fabricated 3-meter purlins , we built three levels of bridges above the passages from 2.5 m height

This space was perfect for storing lightweight items.

The results?

- 6 bridges
- 3 tiers each
- 108 sq. m of brand-new storage area created without occupying any floor space

It was the perfect example of "thinking above the ground."

Key Learnings:

1. A laboratory isn't just a facility or equipment ,it is a symbol of credibility and pride.
2. Reducing unnecessary movement saves time, money, energy, and human effort.
3. There is always room for improvement ,sometimes hidden in plain sight, waiting to be discovered.

Reflections:

The Month of Smoothness, Speed, and Smarter Systems. May reaffirmed something powerful:

A factory doesn't become efficient by adding machines. It becomes efficient when it removes friction and smoothens flow

And in May, we just did that – removed friction and smoothened flow. Five months into 2010, our performance matched the budget exactly. People were motivated. Processes were smooth. ALCO was running with precision and without additional manpower or extra costs.

13

The Month ALCO Stood Tall

Month 11 – June 2010

June arrived with nervous anticipation. The pre-audit visit was scheduled for the first week, and even though the factory had transformed dramatically in just six months, an audit always brings a certain tension.

But something unexpected happened. When the auditor walked through the gates, he stopped. His eyes widened. He looked around like he had stepped into a different world.

The auditor had visited ALCO many times for ISO 9001 audits and knew ALCO. What he saw now was unrecognizable, cleaner, smoother, brighter, and far more organised.

He found a few gaps but his observations sparked new improvements and innovations. June became the month where last-mile changes completed a journey of transformation. A factory once struggling was now confidently preparing to earn its certification.

Change #64: Rescue Lift for Diesel Tank Pit

While touring the premises, the auditor stopped near the diesel tank pit, a massive 100,000-liter underground tank used for the painting line. The pit was 10 meters deep with a ladder leading down. He asked a simple question:

"If someone goes down and collapses, how will you bring them up?"

Silence. We had no answer. That one question showed us how unprepared we were for a crisis. Space around the pit was narrow, barely one meter wide. But instead of seeing a constraint, we saw an opportunity. Within days, we built a sleek rescue cot:

- 70 cm wide
- 1.8 meters long
- Fitted with a lifting winch
- Fully fabricated using in-house material and expertise

Making the in-house lift paid off. The winch came from our sister Factory. The entire setup became another example of ALCO's creativity and resourcefulness. When we tested it, people gathered to watch. The auditor was impressed. And the factory became safer.

Change #65: In-House Eye Wash System

The auditor noticed the aluminium and steel welding activities and questioned how an operator would wash his eyes if something fell in. Goggles and PPE were in use, but he wasn't satisfied. He recommended an eye wash station every 20 meters.

We searched the market and found nothing suitable or economical to overcome this problem. Then our maintenance head came up with a beautiful idea. Using:

- a simple health faucet
- the canopy from our hat-type garden lighting fixture

He created a pedal-operated eye wash system. The operator only had to press the pedal, water shot up gently but forcefully, washing the eyes instantly, and excess water drained through the canopy like a natural funnel. It looked elegant and worked perfectly. Other factories soon gave us orders to supply. Once again, innovation didn't come from budget, it came from brains.

Change #66: The First Smoking Room

The auditor also noticed cigarette stubs around the building. With over 100,000 cartons stored, a single spark could be catastrophic. Smoking was prohibited inside, but employees smoked outside in scattered corners. So ,we created Babtain's first designated smoking room. We converted one of the covered parking spaces near the security cabin:

- partitioned it
- placed chairs
- installed ashtrays
- added a nameplate

Visitors also used it and misuse was minimal. Even non -smokers peeked in to have a look. It was novel , a small change, but it spoke loudly: Safety can be enforced with respect.

Change #67: Redesigning the Design & Planning Office

The Design and Planning team was earlier spread out in small cabins accommodating two persons . Walls isolated them. Communication was slow and the energy was missing. We broke all the partitions and created a large, open hall to accommodate:

- Material planners
- Production planners
- Designers & Draftsmen
- Purchase coordinator

All sitting in visibly connected cubicles with low partitions, just 0.7 meters high. Everyone could see each other. Collaboration became natural. The hall looked modern, spacious, and alive. It was inaugurated with fanfare, the team felt elevated and also felt seen.

Change #68: The Free Coffee Corner

On the first floor, where around 15 executives worked, we added a simple yet powerful morale booster:

- a hot & cold-water dispenser
- tea bags, sugar, cups
- a coffee table with 4 chairs
- a newspaper stands for English and Arabic papers and brochures

The thermostat was reset to ensure water reached 100°C, to enjoy piping hot tea. Soon, not just executives, even shop floor employees began visiting for a cup of tea or to read the paper. A small corner became a melting pot of ideas, relaxation, and bonding.

Change #69: A Fresh Face for ALCO

I always stayed connected with security guards, cleaning boys, drivers, helpers ,shop floor employees and they shared brilliant suggestions without hesitation. They knew the hidden flaws and always wished well for the company without expecting anything in return . Someone came up with an idea to give ALCO a face lift . So, we:

- washed and repainted the building
- tarred the internal roads
- trimmed the trees
- repainted gates and name boards

ALCO did not just function better, it looked better. Visitors began saying, "It feels like a completely different factory." And they were right.

Change #70: Beating the Summer Heat

Summer in Arabia can be merciless with temperatures exceeding 50°C. The shop floor employees requested a soft-drink dispenser to keep their drinks cool . It was a genuine need, not a luxury. We installed it at a prominent spot. Workers stored their drinks and soon the dispenser was full of all sizes and brands of soft drinks and butter milk /curd etc. Laughter, relief, and gratitude filled the area.

Change #71: Vacation Carton Supplies

Employees across the group had a habit of taking ALCO cartons home for packing before vacations. Many demanded cartons "immediately" and wanted the company driver to deliver them. Stores brought it to my notice as it was becoming a nuisance. We couldn't antagonize colleagues, but we also couldn't disrupt operations. So, we implemented a fair system:

1. Kept 200 cartons of two sizes near the security gate.
2. It was to be given on a First come, first served.
3. A register was maintained with security
4. No more personal deliveries.

Some resented the change initially. But once they saw ALCO's performance and discipline, they understood. Over 1000 cartons were saved, and 20–25 extra driver trips were eliminated.

Occasionally, for special cases which was brought to my attention, ALCO supplied them through gate passes signed by me as its not practical to be dogmatic.

Key Learnings:

1. Solutions often exist; it is the manager's responsibility to uncover them.
2. In-house innovation becomes a source of pride, motivation, and unity.

Reflection:

June was a month of maturity where ALCO didn't just work better, it looked better.

Deliveries hit targets again. Every month was an incentive month . Joy was everywhere. People dreamt about earning 14 months of salary. Why not ?

The pre-audit visit was successful. Every observation was attended promptly. The factory looked modern, safe, aesthetic, and efficient, a reflection of the people who built it.

ALCO was no longer just a workplace. It was becoming a model factory.

14

The Month ALCO Bloomed

Month 12 – July 2010

July was unlike any previous month. The heavy lifting was over. The frantic changes were done. The purchase was on autopilot. People knew their roles. Processes were streamlined.

The focus now shifted to the final touches before the audit, paint touch-ups, line marking, polishing, repairs, and countless small details that add up to big impressions. Every apart of the factory was assigned to someone outside that department to ensure fairness and objectivity . Maintenance stood ready to fix whatever was pointed out. Within a week, the factory looked ready, not just for an audit, but for admiration. And then... an idea bloomed. Quite literally.

Change #72: Gardens Bloom in the Desert

With just a week left for the audit, a thought crossed my mind, *"Why don't we do something different and memorable? As it was certification for caring for the environment, why not make the factory green.* In a desert country, greenery is not just decoration, it's emotion, life, and hope. We acted immediately but secretly.

The ALCO Way of Creating Beauty

Using the spinning machine, we crafted round aluminium trays to hold flower pots. We welded inserts at the bottom. Painted them electrostatically to prevent rust. Steel stands and wall brackets were fabricated using scrap from the Pole Factory as base and two-inch pipes. Everything was done in-house, with creativity instead of cost.

The Green Surprise

The evening before the audit, we purchased and placed over 100 potted plants inside and outside the building . The wall mounted brackets were installed on the compound wall while the stands were placed on floor inside the building. The next morning, employees walked into a factory transformed.

- Every 10 meters, a green plant
- Sunlit pots illuminating pathways

Everyone smiled. What was once a functional industrial space now looked like a green sanctuary. It was soothing. Serenity, at its best. ALCO didn't just prepare for an audit; we created an environment that healed the eyes and calmed the mind.

ISO 14000 & OHSAS 18000 Audit

The D-Day arrived. Three factories from our group were scheduled for certification over three days. Because ALCO was the smallest, QA decided to start here. A team of eight officials arrived - auditors, QA coordinators, and safety officers. The moment they entered, their expressions said everything. They didn't expect this! And when they touched the plants and realized they were real, the smiles were priceless.

A Tour Filled with Pride

We walked them through:

- The new lift
- The dust extraction system
- The diesel pit rescue lift
- The storage innovations

- The revamped offices
- The mosque
- The green corridors
- The meticulous housekeeping
- The safety practices in every corner

They were stunned to see safety and environmental control integrated so seamlessly without disrupting production. The Group's QA Manager, known for his strict standards, was speechless. There were no major comments. Just appreciation. We were recommended for both ISO 14000 and OHSAS 18000.

Whose idea? was the regular question from the Auditors and I introduced the originator of the ideas wherever possible. It was a proud and emotional moment for all . Months of sweat, creativity, and courage had led to this day.

Before leaving, the visitors prayed in the mosque, a quiet acknowledgement of respect. And by evening, my counterpart from the High Mast Factory called. "Can I borrow your plants and stands for a day?" Of course, he returned them. But the message was clear, ALCO had set a benchmark.

Key Learnings:

1. A green factory doesn't just please the eyes, it heals minds and lifts spirits.
2. When systems are established and authority is delegated, a company truly runs on autopilot.
3. Give credit where it is due .

Reflection:

With the successful audit:

- Incentives were distributed

- Turnover crossed 25 million Riyals in six months
- Deliveries consistently touched 5 million
- Overtime and incentives filled every pay check with happiness

ALCO was cruising along . What began with chaos a year ago had become a well-oiled, high-performing machine.

But something deeper struck me: For one whole year, we had changed the **factory**, we had changed the systems, and we had changed the lives of people...but we had not yet touched the product or the core processes. That would begin in August.

A new chapter awaited.

Implementation Record:

Sr. No.	Date	Reference change #	Reduce consumption of	Improve Output of	Value

15

Month of Clearing the Old to Make Space for New

Month 13 – August 2010
August 2010 marked one full year since I moved to ALCO and literally witnessed an unbelievable transformation.

The factory now breathed with discipline. Deliveries flowed. Operations were stable. People were confident. But beneath the surface, one silent problem stood like a sore thumb, a non-moving inventory. If ALCO had to evolve to the next level, the clutter had to go. August became the month of courage, the courage to discard the past to make room for the future.

Change #73: Reducing SKUs by Writing Off Obsolete Inventory

On the 1st of August, the ERP system revealed a shocking number: 3300+ SKU's in stores. That meant:

- three thousand + of unique items
- hundreds of unused components
- duplications
- wrong supplies
- items untouched for over a year
- and valuable space consumed with zero return

The stores looked full, but full of what? No movement of material. No purpose in the presence. Just... material that had lost its relevance. We decided to confront it. A senior employee, someone who knew the store well was tasked to identify obsolete SKU's.

A Leadership Decision with Long-Term Courage

Writing off inventory is a sensitive topic in any organisation. It can create fear, questions, even resistance. The blame game would start and never end

But management showed courage and pragmatism . They agreed to write off a fixed value of obsolete inventory every month for the next three years, so that:

- profitability would remain unaffected
- stores could gradually be cleared
- mistakes of the past would not choke the future

And so it began, month after month, the obsolete list was reviewed, approved, and removed. Space opened. Clarity returned. The store looked younger. Letting go is painful. But sometimes, letting go is what allows progress to walk in.

Change #74: Part Commonization and Standardization

ALCO manufactured so many models, that the number of unique parts had exploded. But did we really need such complexity? Most parts were similar in function, but with slight variations in:

- length
- thickness
- hole sizes
- finish

Complexity had crept in silently over the years, adding:

- more SKUs
- more purchasing
- more handling and storing
- more room for errors

We decided to simplify.

A Three-Month Mission

- The Design Department was assigned a clear mission:
- Identify parts that could be standardised
- Combine similar components
- Reduce variations without affecting performance
- Create a lean, common parts library
- Help reduce SKUs dramatically

It was not just a design task. It was a mindset shift from "every model is different" to "let's build smarter, not harder." This journey laid the foundation for future improvements where even the product itself would undergo transformation.

Key Learnings:

1. There are countless ways to improve, if only we dare to open our eyes.
2. Identifying improvement opportunities is not a task; it is the responsibility of the leader at the top.

Reflection:

August brought not just operational clarity, but also a prestigious victory. We won a major project to illuminate the Makkah-Madina railway line, the first railway line in the Western Province of Saudi Arabia.

Millions of pilgrims would travel this route. The project was highly public, highly competitive, and time-sensitive.

Delivery deadline: November 30. Pressure level: extreme. But ALCO was ready. Because our systems were strong and people were motivated. Meanwhile:

- Painting, assembly, housekeeping all operated smoothly
- SKU reduction efforts picked up momentum
- Ramadan arrived, bringing blessings and a quieter, reflective atmosphere
- And one full year of transformation at ALCO was completed

August ended just like the previous months with deliveries above 5 million. But beneath that stability, a deeper shift was beginning. The focus was moving from fixing the factory to elevating the product. A new phase awaited.

16

The Month of Quiet Refinement

Month 14 – September 2010

September arrived wrapped in the spirit of Ramadan. It was a month of reflection both spiritually and operationally. The blistering heat of the Arabian summer had kept major changes on pause, but in ALCO, the momentum never truly stopped.

Iftar meet had become a tradition, and this year's Iftar held on the 5th of September, was no different. It was warm, heartfelt, and well attended. They knew what to expect . People came together like a family. The factory felt united, connected, and proud. The plants had grown. With one more quarter remaining, we were well on track to achieve something ALCO had never accomplished before:

50 million riyals in a single year.

A milestone that once seemed distant was now within touching distance. But even as we celebrated, we knew one truth -progress doesn't pause. Many of the improvements made over the past year were now revisited not out of necessity, but out of commitment. We didn't want a lull, even after certification. The culture of continuous improvement had taken root.

Change 75: Downsizing Motors in the Painting Line

The painting line had five preparation chambers ,each spraying chemicals or water solutions when the objects passed through them. Each chamber used a 5 HP motor to pump the solution.

Observing the plant performance one day, noted the big motor sizes . Back home in India we used 1 HP motors for pumping water from the well to the tank on the first floor where the lift was over 50 feet . Here the lift was hardly 20 feet and we were using 5 HP motors. Why? There was no logical answer. We consulted a Siemens engineer from Riyadh. He inspected the system and then smiled gently:

"Perhaps, years ago, > 1 < 5 HP options weren't available. Someone chose 5 HP for convenience and ... 1 Hp was risky ."

Convenience from the past had now become unnecessary cost. He recommended 2 HP motors, but we decided to try with a 3 HP, a practical middle ground that was readily available.

The Secret Experiment

We replaced one motor on a Friday , without informing QC to avoid any interference or preconceived objections. For two days, we watched the output. Hour after hour. Fitting after fitting and then... we relaxed. No rejection, no remarks. It worked perfectly. In the following weeks, all five motors were replaced correctly and officially through the IOR system. **The Result:**

- Power reduction: **10 HP**
- Saving: **7.4 units per hour**
- Monthly saving: **4,290 units**
- Annual saving: **51,480 units**

A simple change. A thoughtful decision. A massive recurring saving. It was a decision arising from curiosity and it worked very well.

Change 76: In-House Cleaning of Heat Exchanger Tubes

The pressure die-casting plant, 50 km away had always struggled with breakdowns. Overheating was a familiar enemy. In September, a major breakdown disrupted the entire planning cycle. The heat exchanger had clogged, choking the system. A professional cleaning team demanded an exorbitant amount and extensive downtime. Instead of surrendering, we got creative.

We transported the heat exchanger to our anodising unit. There, the supervisor and his assistant began cleaning it using chemicals while the maintenance team joined the act and drilled through blocked tubes wherever possible. Initially, the exchanger could hold only 0.5 litres of coolant. After two days of cleaning, it held 5 litres. A tenfold improvement. A crisis turned into a quiet triumph. Once again, in-house innovation saved the day.

Key Learning:

1. Every day and every month bring their own challenges, what matters is the courage and clarity with which we face them.

Reflection:

Despite the relentless heat and many employees still on vacation, September ended as another successful month. On the evening of September 30th, after office hours, I received a call from my boss.

"Let's meet for coffee in the High Mast factory tomorrow morning," he said. "Come with the Operation Manager... and bring the file of the mega project we received in August."

I instantly sensed it: The delivery deadline might be advanced.

Perhaps to mid-November. Perhaps even earlier.

The next month was going to test every ounce of ALCO's capability.

But that is what leadership is about; meeting challenges the moment they arise.

17

The Month of the Impossible

Month 15 – October 2010

October didn't begin; it exploded into action. By 7.30 , we arrived at the High Mast factory office. The atmosphere was tense. Along with me and the Operation Manager, the Tower Factory Manager was present too. All three of us reported to the same DGM. Something big was coming and we could feel it. DGM entered, greeted everyone politely, and then delivered the blow with calm authority:

"Bandar Jeddah Project must be delivered completely by 15th October. I know it's difficult, but we have to do it. All resources are at your disposal. My doors are open. Meeting over."

He walked out. We sat frozen. Fifteen days. For a project of that magnitude. It was almost unreal. But leadership is not about questioning difficulty, it is about answering it.

Change #77: Get the Specs Changed to Meet Delivery

Our scope included Floodlights , Luminaires ,over hundred distribution boxes for High Masts and close to thousand fuse boxes for poles . We immediately checked the status of every component and a nightmare unfolded:

- Some were still in Europe
- Some in India
- Some in China

- Local suppliers promised supply in early November

Most items could be air-freighted, except for one floodlight . It was to illuminate the stations and was short by 700 pieces. We tried everything including borrowing from contractors but Nothing worked. That's when the Design and PPC team sprang into action. Hours of brainstorming led to a bold idea:

Could we check the optics from an underpass fitting available in stock instead? The underpass fitting was unrelated to the original requirement but worth trying. To everyone's surprise:

- Optics matched
- Light Output and distribution matched

The only difference? The underpass fitting was extruded aluminium while the original specification called for die cast aluminium. It was technically sound, operationally feasible but commercially expensive. Visited HO, met with the DGM, and he approved the extra cost instantly. Sales moved quickly, met the client in Jeddah , the consultant, and the project authorities. Even though the fitting was more expensive, the contractor insisted that pricing must remain unchanged. As management had approved, we accepted the variation. We were happy to contribute to a noble cause and ensure safety for the millions of pilgrims traveling between Makkah and Madina during Haj 2010.

15 Days of Fire, Focus, and Unshakeable Will

The project which should've taken two months was completed in 15 days**.** The company supported wholeheartedly: Employees gave their heart out working from 6 am to 9 pm . To ease their load company provided:

- Evening dinner
- Laundry facilities

- Snacks ,tea when needed

The last trailer left on 15th October, exactly as demanded. On 17th October, management gave a special bonus to both factories.

This was the second bonus of the month, the fourth of the year, and yet another one was coming. ALCO had achieved the unthinkable.

Change #78: Family Day

To honour the team's extraordinary effort, a grand Family Day was organised the very next Friday.

A large farmhouse was booked. The entire ALCO family arrived with their spouses and children. People laughed, played, relaxed and it was a day of pure joy. Activities like Volleyball , football and swimming filled the air with energy:

A lavish lunch was dished out and friends from other factories joined too.

By afternoon, a live orchestra began. Hindi, Malayalam, Tamil, Arabic songs echoed through the farmland. As per Saudi norms, female singers weren't allowed, but a 10-year-old boy stole the show with his angelic voice. Employees came forward to sing, crack jokes because on that day, there were no workers or managers. We were one family, celebrating a victory earned with sweat, sacrifice, and unity. It was the first Family Day in the group's history.

Key Learnings:

1. "Impossible" is just another way of saying "I am possible."
2. Every organisation hides unused capacity waiting to be unlocked by a challenge.
3. Alternatives always exist; you just have to look where others don't.

Reflection:

October was a month that tested ALCO's courage, creativity, and collective strength. What began as an ordinary morning turned into one of the biggest challenges in ALCO's history and we delivered the massive Bandar Jeddah Project in just 15 days. It was like being in a battlefield. Not a dull moment .

Against all odds, the team rose like never before. October was the month ALCO recognised its extraordinary power.

And Dispatch? It didn't just break delivery records; it became the mother of all months.

Implementation Record:

Sr. No.	Date	Reference change #	Reduce consumption of	Improve Output of	Value

18

The Month of Hidden Treasures and New Horizons

Month 16 – November 2010

The first ten months of 2010 at ALCO felt nothing short of a fairy tale. A factory once struggling was now cruising at full throttle. We had crossed last year's dispatch value with ease and were now heading confidently toward 50 million riyals, a milestone unmatched in the company's history.

And then came the bigger question whispering in every corridor: *"Will we touch 10 million in profits?"* The possibility felt bold, exciting...but not within reach.

November became a month of discoveries some planned, some accidental, and each one added to the momentum that was carrying ALCO to its best-ever year.

Change #79: Unearthing a Copper Mine

Inside the factory, between two lattice supports at the centre of the building, were a few covered storage racks with locks. These were used years ago to keep tools and valuable items. They sat quietly in a corner, unnoticed.

One day, for reasons still unknown, we tried to move them but they wouldn't budge. The key was missing too. So, we decided to shift the storage rack using the big forklift. When we finally opened it, what we saw left us stunned. Almost Eight tons of copper bus bars.

ALCO used to manufacture substation panels nearly a decade ago, and these were remnants of that old business. Copper prices had skyrocketed. The difference between the old cost and the current market price was massive. Selling the bus bars gave us a clean profit windfall.

And I remembered Paulo Coelho's famous line from *The Alchemist*: *"When you want something, all the universe conspires in helping you achieve it."* I mentioned this quote in the opening chapter of the book as well. We weren't looking for treasure. But treasure found us.

Change #80: Standardizing High Mast Distribution Boxes

Every high mast requires an internal distribution box, carefully designed to operate the luminaires and the winch. But for years, each project meant a new drawing. Every order, was tailor made and a fresh design was submitted for approval. More than 500 different drawings existed! This chaos created:

- Long delivery times
- Complex procurement
- Unpredictable planning
- Higher costs

So, we brought the Pole Factory Manager into the discussion. The DB designer joined us and immediately understood the issue.

Within a short period, he standardised the entire DB line, reducing 500 models to just 10 types, good enough for 80% of the orders. The Pareto principle worked beautifully. This single move transformed everything:

- procurement became easier
- delivery became faster

- costs reduced
- sales surged further

High Mast sales were booming, and with the new standardized DBs, ALCO gained a consistent contributor to monthly revenue. Standardization didn't just simplify manufacturing, it amplified performance.

Change #81: Adding Colours to Luminaires

ALCO's standard luminaire colour was grey. Whenever customers asked for other colours, we refused not by choice, but because the process was painful. To switch colour:

1. Stop the entire line.
2. Recover expensive powder paint from painting chamber
3. Clean the bag filter and gun
4. Load the new colour and trial run .
5. After production, repeat everything to return to grey

Total downtime: 5 to 6 hours. Lost opportunity? Even greater. Many customers were willing to pay extra for special colours but we weren't able to serve them. The bottleneck was the single bag filter. So, we moved quickly:

- Purchased 2 sets of filter bags
- Fabricated new bag filter housings in-house, copying the original
- Implemented a simple swapping system

Now, whenever a colour change was required, the bag house could be replaced instantly. Downtime dropped from 6 hours to under 30 minutes. Suddenly:

- Any colour could be supplied

- Customers were delighted
- New business opportunities opened up
- Flexibility became a strength

What we once saw as a constraint became a competitive advantage.

Key Learnings:

1. Adding colours is not just aesthetics; it opens doors to new markets and new demand.
2. Challenges and opportunities are two sides of the same coin, what we call a problem is often the beginning of discovery.

Reflection:

By now, ALCO was a machine that ran on rhythm, confidence, and clarity.

Delivery was flawless, on time. Material flowed smoothly. Every face radiated pride and positivity. And for the first time, I felt something unusual.

I had nothing major to do. The factory was running itself. That is the reward of leadership: building a system that works even when you're not watching.

19

Month of Discipline, Control & a Historic Finish

Month 17 – December 2010

December arrived not as the end of the year, but as the grand finale of one of the greatest transformations ALCO had ever seen. From chaos to clarity. From survival to stability. From uncertainty to record-breaking performance.

By now, ALCO was no longer just working well, it was performing like a world-class organisation. Large Orders , for thousand or more pieces was coming in consistently. Customers and utilities had begun to trust ALCO without hesitation. The respect we earned was visible in every PO that arrived. But big orders come with their own big challenges.

Change #82: Produce Only One Trailer or One Container Load

With massive orders, a new problem surfaced: Stock was piling up. Material would be ready, but dispatch would be delayed due to:

- Third-party inspections
- Site readiness issues
- Client delays

And when finished goods sit idle, they choke cash flow and occupy precious space. So, we made a bold, simple, and brilliant rule:

Produce only one trailer-load (or container-load) at a time. Dispatch it. Then produce the next. Not earlier. Not in bulk. Just in rhythm.

Many customers tried to persuade us:

"Invoice it, but keep it there. We'll take it later."

We stood firm. ISO procedures didn't allow it was our reply. And once ISO is quoted clients embrace silence. It worked beautifully.

- Open trailer → 400 luminaires
- Closed container → 360 luminaires
- Quantities varied by model

Soon, customers began appreciating this system too, as it helped them avoid unnecessary stocking. It was a win-win situation without compromise.

Change #83: Reducing the Width of the Unloading Bay

The unloading bay at ALCO was 4 metres wide. Appeared good on paper but in reality, it caused delays every single day especially when part loads arrived. Because:

- Materials could only be unloaded from the back
- If the part load was placed deeper inside the trailer, the unloading bay could not be used. Trailers had to park inside the premises and unload happened from the side.

This slowed movement, and created delay. So we redesigned the unloading bay by:

- Reducing the bay width to 2.5 metres.

- Built a side platform so forklifts could enter from the side of an open trailer

This one change made unloading incredibly smooth:

- Faster
- Safer
- No more unloading in the open area

It helped especially during the frequent arrival of carton from domestic suppliers. It was the change that created a big relief.

Key Learnings:

1. Small structural changes can unlock big operational advantages.
2. Every achievement is the result of collective strength, not individual brilliance.
3. Variety and variations add to the cost

Reflection:
By the time December ended:

- SKU count was dropping fast
- On time delivery was above 95%
- Turnaround time improved

And the final numbers told the story louder than words could:
Turnover: SR 54 million
Profit: SR 10.4 million
The highest ever. A figure that once felt impossible and now stood proudly in our books. As I reflected on the journey, a wave of gratitude washed over me. This miracle wasn't mine alone. It belonged to every soul who walked through ALCO's gates.

- My boss who trusted me
- Top Management who supported every bold step
- Sales, who brought the orders
- Purchase, who ensured every part arrived on time
- Accounts, who kept us financially grounded
- QA & QC, who safeguarded quality
- Stores, who reorganised their world
- Civil, Maintenance, Planning, PPC, Drivers, Security, everyone

Every person, from senior managers to the newest helper on the night shift, worked with heart, discipline, and belief. It was a transformation powered not by machines, but by human commitment. And in that moment, I could only say one thing:

"Thank you, God, for giving me the chance to witness and lead this journey."

The year didn't just end. It closed like a chapter of destiny, a story of faith, courage, unity, and relentless improvement. A story that would stay with me forever.

Implementation Record:

Sr. No.	Date	Reference change #	Reduce consumption of	Improve Output of	Value

20

A Journey From Uncertainty to Star Performer

What began with trepidation, doubt, and the fear of the unknown slowly transformed into one of the most rewarding journeys of my life. The opportunity to touch so many lives...
to raise the income of more than 200 employees...
to replace worry with pride...
to replace helplessness with hope...
And that was the greatest victory of all.

When I look back at the seventeen months at ALCO, one truth stands out clearly:

Change is not the enemy. Change is the path. Change is the only constant that guarantees progress. The changes we made were profound. Some were bold, some were small, some were invisible, some were repeated quietly until they took root. Many more changes happened beyond these pages, some too simple to record, others too repetitive to describe. But each one, like a droplet of water, contributed to a rising tide.

A tide that turned a struggling factory into a profitable, proud, high-performing organisation. A tide that strengthened the culture, discipline, and confidence of every employee. A tide that transformed ALCO, not through theory, but through action.

And remarkably...This turnaround did not require:

- Expensive consultants
- Popular philosophies like Lean, TOC, or Six Sigma
- Overworking people or machines
- Downsizing or job cuts
- Endless analysis
- Psychological restructuring
- Nor forcing behavioural change

Instead, it was built upon:

- **Actions** - simple, continuous, relentless
- **People welfare** - because cared people care more
- **Observation and attention** - noticing what others ignored
- **Discussions and consensus** - solutions born through unity
- **Respect for every stakeholder** - owners, employees, suppliers, customers, and society
- **Systemic changes** - the kind that make success repeatable and automatic
- **Fun, laughter, music, and celebrations**

This was not a miracle. It was a human transformation, rooted in commitment and collective spirit. These seventeen months proved something powerful. When you improve the system, the system improves the people. When you uplift people, they uplift the organisation. And when both align excellence becomes inevitable.

My hope is that this book does more than share ideas. May it inspire you, challenge you, and encourage you to believe that real change is possible - faster, simpler, and more joyfully than you ever imagined. May it guide you to:

- Bring lasting improvements to your organisation
- Increase profitability without stress
- Deliver on time without chaos

- Reduce waste without complication
- And most importantly, enhance the lives of your employees, who are the true heartbeat of every enterprise.

If ALCO could rise, so can any organisation. All it takes is the courage to begin, and the consistency to continue. May your journey be filled with impact, abundance, and transformation.

21

The 17-Month Transformation Roadmap

Month	Change Number	Change Title
Month 1 – Aug 2009	1	A Strategic Leap of Faith
Month 1 – Aug 2009	2	When You Decide to Change, Embrace It Fully
Month 1 – Aug 2009	3	Some Storms Come to Clear the Path
Month 2 – Sep 2009	4	A Seat That Changed Perspective
Month 2 – Sep 2009	5	The Paradigm Shift - From Production to Delivery
Month 2 – Sep 2009	6	Fostering Relationships - Iftar at ALCO
Month 2 – Sep 2009	7	Closer Surveillance Through CCTV

Month 2 – Sep 2009	8	Moving Setup Time Outside the Shift
Month 2 – Sep 2009	9	Establishing a Disagreement Mechanism
Month 2 – Sep 2009	10	Cobweb-Free Factory
Month 3 – Oct 2009	11	Arrive Early, Leave Early
Month 3 – Oct 2009	12	Sharing Performance with Shop Floor Employees
Month 3 – Oct 2009	13	Aging Bucket for Stock
Month 3 – Oct 2009	14	Objective-Based Inventory Management
Month 3 – Oct 2009	15	A Discounted New Price List
Month 3 – Oct 2009	16	Sustainability Practices
Month 3 – Oct 2009	17	Removing Items Not in Inventory
Month 3 – Oct 2009	18	Reduce Work in Process
Month 3 – Oct 2009	19	The Employee Dining Hall

Month 3 – Oct 2009	20	Clean Drinking Water
Month 3 – Oct 2009	21	A Kennel for the Dogs
Month 3 – Oct 2009	22	Tea for All
Month 4 – Nov 2009	23	Production Bonus
Month 4 – Nov 2009	24	Skylights: Letting the Sun Back In
Month 4 – Nov 2009	25	Introducing Job Rotation for Supervisors
Month 4 – Nov 2009	26	Retiring Models That No Longer Served the Business
Month 4 – Nov 2009	27	Removing Siesta Joints- Reclaiming Discipline
Month 4 – Nov 2009	28	Petty Cash Purchases: The Hidden Drain on Profit
Month 4 – Nov 2009	29	Disciplinary Action- A Necessary Storm
Month 5 – Dec 2009	30	Freeze the Production Plan

Month 5 – Dec 2009	31	Vacation Is to Be Availed, Not Accumulated
Month 5 – Dec 2009	32	Decision to Pursue ISO Certification
Month 5 – Dec 2009	33	Buying a Drivable Floor-Cleaning Machine
Month 5 – Dec 2009	34	Farewells That End with Happiness
Month 5 – Dec 2009	35	Visitor Badges-Stopping Hidden Disruptions
Month 5 – Dec 2009	36	The Hissing Sound - A Silent Power Drain
Month 5 – Dec 2009	37	Appraisals and the Forced Distribution Challenge
Month 5 – Dec 2009	38	The Audacious 2010 Budget
Month 6 – Jan 2010	39	The Cost-Reduction Project - A Collective Promise
Month 6 – Jan 2010	40	Reorganising Electrical Assembly - Traceability Equals Trust

Month 6 – Jan 2010	41	Certification - A Punch List and a Promise
Month 6 – Jan 2010	42	Resetting Stores - Think Vertical, Not Just Horizontal
Month 6 – Jan 2010	43	Use Stock with Modification – Innovate
Month 6 – Jan 2010	44	Closing Half the Gate - Reclaiming Space
Month 6 – Jan 2010	45	Specify Rejection Criteria - End the Tug-of-War with QC
Month 6 – Jan 2010	46	Publishing the Rationale for Increments - Transparency Heals
Month 7 – Feb 2010	47	Bulk Ordering with Heart and Foresight
Month 7 – Feb 2010	48	The Paint that Flaked—and the Lesson that Shined
Month 7 – Feb 2010	49	The Showroom That Told Our Story
Month 8 – Mar 2010	50	Quarterly Incentive Linked to Dispatch

Month 8 – Mar 2010	51	Rethinking the Inside Paint
Month 8 – Mar 2010	52	The Wire Cutting Machine and others
Month 8 – Mar 2010	53	The Home-Made Lift
Month 8 – Mar 2010	54	The Home-Made Dust Extraction System
Month 9 – Apr 2010	55	Painting Line Overhaul
Month 9 – Apr 2010	56	The Mosque Modification
Month 9 – Apr 2010	57	Create Space Out of Thin Air
Month 9 – Apr 2010	58	Reducing Chemical Store Size
Month 10 – May 2010	59	The Real-Time Packing Report
Month 10 – May 2010	60	Moving the IP Lab
Month 10 – May 2010	61	Setting Right the Fouling Cable Trays
Month 10 – May 2010	62	Reducing Material Travel Distance
Month 10 – May 2010	63	Bridging the Racks

Month 11 – Jun 2010	64	Rescue Lift for Diesel Tank Pit
Month 11 – Jun 2010	65	In-House Eye Wash System
Month 11 – Jun 2010	66	The First Smoking Room
Month 11 – Jun 2010	67	Redesigning the Design & Planning Office
Month 11 – Jun 2010	68	The Free Coffee Corner
Month 11 – Jun 2010	69	A Fresh Face for ALCO
Month 11 – Jun 2010	70	Beating the Summer Heat
Month 11 – Jun 2010	71	Vacation Carton Supplies
Month 12 – Jul 2010	72	Gardens Bloom in the Desert
Month 13 – Aug 2010	73	Reducing SKUs by Writing Off Obsolete Inventory
Month 13 – Aug 2010	74	Part Commonization and Standardization

Month 14 – Sep 2010	75	Downsizing Motors in the Painting Line
Month 14 – Sep 2010	76	In-House Cleaning of Heat Exchanger Tubes
Month 15 – Oct 2010	77	Get the Specs Changed to Meet Delivery
Month 15 – Oct 2010	78	Family Day
Month 16 – Nov 2010	79	Unearthing a Copper Mine
Month 16 – Nov 2010	80	Standardizing High Mast Distribution Boxes
Month 16 – Nov 2010	81	Adding Colours to Luminaires
Month 17 – Dec 2010	82	Produce Only One Trailer or One Container Load
Month 17 – Dec 2010	83	Reducing the Width of the Unloading Bay

22

Find Me Here

LinkedIn

https://www.linkedin.com/in/ninan-chandy-5833b810/

DELTAETA COST REDUCTION CONSULTANTS PVT. LTD.

https://deltaeta.in/

Amazon Book QR Code

9 789356 021242

Printed at Repro India Ltd.